Jack R. Fraenkel/ Enoch I. Sawin/ Norman E. Wallen

VISUAL STATISTICS
A Conceptual Primer

Allyn and Bacon

Boston / London / Toronto / Sydney / Tokyo / Singapore

To Marge, Lina, and Barbara for a LOT of patience while we worked on this book.

Editorial Assistant: Mark Listenik
Editorial-Production Service: Kathy Smith
Art Studio: Schneck-DePippo Graphics
Interior Design: Melinda Grosser, for *silk*
Cover Administrator: Brian Gogolin
Composition Buyer: Linda Cox
Manufacturing Buyer: Suzanne Lareau

Copyright © 1999 by Allyn & Bacon
A Viacom Company
160 Gould Street
Needham Heights, MA 02494

Internet: www.abacon.com

All rights reserved. No part of the material protected by this copyright notice may be reproduced or utilized in any form or by any means, electronic or mechanical, including photocopying, recording, or by any information storage or retrieval system, without written permission from the copyright owner.

Library of Congress Cataloging-in-Publication Data

Fraenkel, Jack R.
    Visual statistics : a conceptual primer / Jack R. Fraenkel, Enoch
  I. Sawin, Norman E. Wallen.
        p.   cm.
    Includes bibliographical references and index.
    ISBN 0-205-28317-9
    1. Mathematical statistics.   2. Mathematical statistics—Charts,
  diagrams, etc.   I. Sawin, Enoch I.   II. Wallen, Norman E.
    III. Title.
  QA276.18.F7   1999
  519.5—dc21   98-27531
                                                        CIP

Printed in the United States of America
10 9 8 7 6 5 4 3 2 1   04 03 02 99 98

Contents

Organizing and Summarizing Data

SET 2 Tables, Graphs, and Distributions 49

SET 3 Centers and Spreads (Summary Measures) 79

SET 4 Measurement 105

PART III

Experimentation

Looking for Relationships in Data

Contents vii

SET 7 Relationships between Quantitative Variables: Regression 209

SET 8 Relationships between Categorical Variables 227

Drawing Conclusions from Data

SET 9 Probability 243

SET 10 Inferential Reasoning 273

Appendix Contents 324

Preface

This is not a textbook. Although it includes most of the terms and ideas you will find in almost all introductory statistics texts, we do not discuss them at length. Rather, we describe them very briefly (sometimes in only a few sentences) and then follow these descriptions with one or two examples and illustrations.

We had three purposes in writing this book:

- To help you understand and even enjoy many of the more important ideas in statistics. To do this, we used a variety of illustrations, ranging from cartoons to graphs to tables.
- To demystify statistical terms and methods. Traditional statistics books often place too much emphasis on computation and not enough on understanding. In this book, we take just the opposite approach.
- To show you how statistics applies to real life. In this regard, we offer abundant examples from a variety of fields to illustrate how statistics and statistical methods are used in everyday affairs. Examples include anthropology, biology, business economics, education, environmental science, forestry, geology, linguistics, medicine, meteorology, pharmacology, psychology, government, political science, sociology, and sports.

Above all, we think the study of statistics should be interesting. Accordingly, we have tried to make it so. Only a few of the very simplest kinds of formulas are provided in the main part of the book. But for those who think they need (or want) more, we have provided in the appendices and with computational examples, some of the more commonly used formulas. We provide near the end of the book a selected bibliography of more traditionally designed and organized introductory statistics textbooks.

Let us say a few words about the illustrations that we include in the book. Almost all of the concepts in the book are illustrated by means of a drawing, cartoon, graph, chart, or table. Almost all of these illustrations are original, and they are the unique feature of the book. Our intent, again, throughout the book is to emphasize understanding, rather than calculation.

Please note that the concepts are presented sequentially within each section. We have done this to enable you to refer to the concepts in approximately the same order as they are found in most introductory statistics texts. We also provide an alphabetical list of the concepts in each section at the beginning of the section.

You will notice that many (we hope most) of the concepts are quite easy to understand in and of themselves. A few, however, are somewhat more advanced and more difficult to comprehend without first studying one or two (sometimes even three or four) of the other, more elementary concepts. Should you find the description of a concept, or its illustration, difficult to understand, reviewing the concepts listed after the heading "See Also" is helpful.

We are grateful to our reviewers—Kayte Perry, Oklahoma State University and Glenn Graham, Wright State University—for their thoughtful and helpful suggestions.

Finally, we wish to emphasize that, unless otherwise noted, all of our examples are fictitious. They do not represent real data, although real data would be analyzed in similar, and often identical, ways.

We hope you find the book interesting, useful, and even, yes, fun to read!

JRF
EIS
NEW

SAMPLING
PART I

Set 1

Sampling is essential in statistics, for it is rarely possible to obtain information on all of the members of an entire population of individuals. As a result, scientists, pollsters, and other researchers select a *sample*, or subgroup of individuals from a population of interest and then draw conclusions about that population on the basis of what they discover about the sample. As a wit once said, "You don't have to eat the whole cow to know the meat is rotten!" This is the basic idea of sampling: To draw conclusions about the whole of something by studying only a part of it. In this section we describe and illustrate several of the more important concepts involved in sampling.

Samples, Sampling, and Sampling Distributions

Listed Sequentially

assumption
population/sample
generalizability
unit
sampling frame
variable
constant
statistic/parameter
margin of error
descriptive statistics
inferential statistics
representative sample
random sampling
table of random numbers
cluster random sample
stratified random sample
convenience sample
purposive sample
systematic sample
multistage sampling
sampling distribution
sampling error
sampling with and without replacement

Listed Alphabetically

assumption
cluster random sample
constant
convenience sample
descriptive statistics
generalizability
inferential statistics
margin of error
multistage sampling
population/sample
purposive sample
random sampling
representative sample
sampling distribution
sampling error
sampling frame
sampling with and without replacement
statistic/parameter
stratified random sample
systematic sample
table of random numbers
unit
variable

Assumption

Description An **assumption** is a statement that is taken for granted, that is, presumed to be true without evidence being presented for testing or checking it. It is a proposition from which a sequence of reasoning begins. All reasoning involves assumptions. Some are impossible to test; some might be possible to test at some future time but are stated with the knowledge that they are subject to challenge. Many statistical techniques, such as analysis of variance or regression analysis, require that certain assumptions be made about the data. Some of the most important involve sampling. Violations of these assumptions can lead to misleading or even meaningless results.

Example Survey research conclusions are sometimes based on the assumption that the people who are interviewed answered questions honestly. However, it is almost impossible to find out whether they are telling the truth. An example might be a survey in which husbands in two-income families are asked about the extent to which they perform cooking, cleaning, child care, and other household chores. Some of the husbands interviewed might exaggerate the amount of housework they do. A few might be too embarrassed to admit that they do as much as they actually do. In any survey, there is no certain way of knowing how many of the people who are interviewed distorted the truth and, if so, by how much.

FIGURE 1.1 ARE THESE ASSUMPTIONS WARRANTED?

Population/Sample

Description   A **population** includes all of the members of a particular group of individuals (events, organizations, institutions, or other subjects being studied) that one wishes to describe or about which one wishes to generalize. It is usually very difficult (and often impossible) to study the entire population. Most populations of interest are quite large, diverse, and spread over a large geographic area. Finding, let alone contacting, all of the members of a population can be very time consuming and expensive. Therefore, one often studies a *sample* (a subgroup) that is thought (or meant) to be *representative* of the population. When objects are being studied, the term *universe* is often used instead of population.

Examples
- All of the police officers in the United States
- All of the lawyers in the state of Alaska
- All of the trees in Detroit, Michigan
- All of the students in Ms. Johnson's third-grade class at Potrero Elementary School
- All of the registered voters in San Mateo, California
- All of the owners of telephones in the state of Nevada
- All of the households in which Washington High School students live

See also   Convenience sample; purposive sample; random sampling; representative sample; unit.

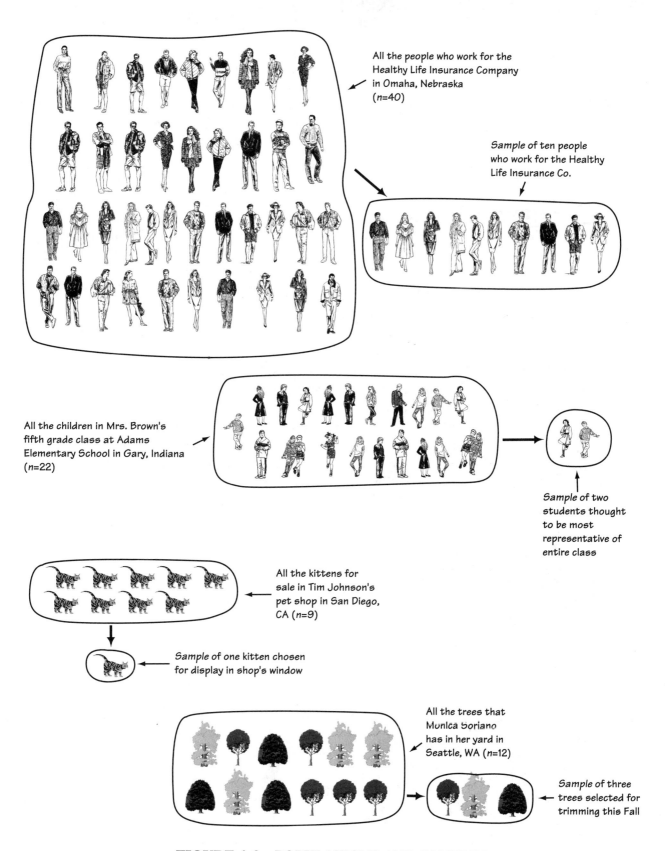

All the people who work for the Healthy Life Insurance Company in Omaha, Nebraska (*n*=40)

Sample of ten people who work for the Healthy Life Insurance Co.

All the children in Mrs. Brown's fifth grade class at Adams Elementary School in Gary, Indiana (*n*=22)

Sample of two students thought to be most representative of entire class

All the kittens for sale in Tim Johnson's pet shop in San Diego, CA (*n*=9)

Sample of one kitten chosen for display in shop's window

All the trees that Monica Soriano has in her yard in Seattle, WA (*n*=12)

Sample of three trees selected for trimming this Fall

FIGURE 1.2 POPULATIONS AND SAMPLES

Population/Sample   **5**

Generalizability

Description **Generalizability** is the extent or degree to which you can come to a conclusion about a population based on information obtained from a sample.

Examples

- Suppose that the executives of a large department store chain want to see whether a new line of women's clothing will sell. Accordingly, they try out the new line in a few selected stores in various cities that they assume are representative of the United States as a whole. If the line sells well and their assumption is correct, the executives can generalize from the sales in the few selected stores to how well the line will sell in the rest of the country.

- A college administrator selects a random sample of 250 students from the sophomore class of 1500 students at a large university in North Carolina. This sample of students is surveyed concerning their views about the quality of campus housing for students. Since the sample was randomly selected, the administrator intends to use the results of the survey as a basis for drawing some conclusions about the views of the entire sophomore class on this issue.

See also Inferential statistics.

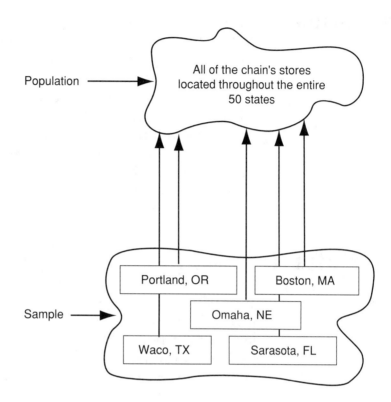

FIGURE 1.3   GENERALIZING FROM A SAMPLE

Unit

Description
The term **unit** is used in several different ways in statistics. One use refers to the individual members (e.g., individuals, objects, documents, or regions) that make up a population. If the population consists of people, the members are often called *subjects*.

A second use refers to experiments and observations. Experimental units are the smallest objects to which a researcher can assign different treatments in an experiment. Observational units are the objects being observed. When the units in an experiment or observation are humans, they are, again, called subjects (or sometimes participants).

Examples
- In a survey of adults (age 18 and over) living in households in the state of Texas, the unit would be any adult living in the state who is over 18 years of age (but excluding individuals in institutions such as prisons or mental hospitals). In such a large, highly populated state, the procedure would probably be to select a random sample of adults to interview, rather than go to the expense of collecting the data from every adult in the state.

- A professor at a large midwestern university wants to investigate student attitudes toward the use of marijuana. She decides to use a sample of 100 students, selected from all the freshman students at the university. She obtains a list of all the 550 freshmen who are studying psychology and chooses a simple random sample of 100 of the 550 students on the list. The unit in this case is any individual freshman psychology student.

See also Experiment; observational study; population/sample.

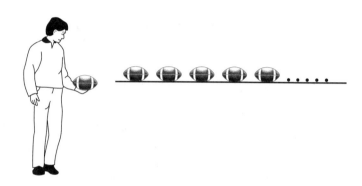

(b) A quality control engineer checking the size of footballs as they come off a production line in a sports equipment plant. The unit is any football.

FIGURE 1.4   UNITS

Sampling Frame

Description   A **sampling frame** is a list or other record of the population from which we draw a sample.

Examples
- Suppose a researcher wanted to select a sample from all of the residents of a large city. If she picked every 100th name listed in the city telephone directory, the directory would be the sampling frame.

  It is to be desired that the sampling frame include *all* of the members of the population, but this almost never occurs. In the example just given, some people will not have a telephone. Others may not be listed in the directory. Still others may be listed in the directory but have since moved to another city.

- A high school teacher uses her class list to select five students to participate in an after-school assembly. Her class list is the sampling frame.

- Suppose that statistics are collected on a sample of all starting professional baseball pitchers in the National League who have pitched at least four innings in three or more games during the 1998 season. The sampling frame would be the list of those pitchers.

See also   Convenience sample; population/sample; purposive sample; random sampling.

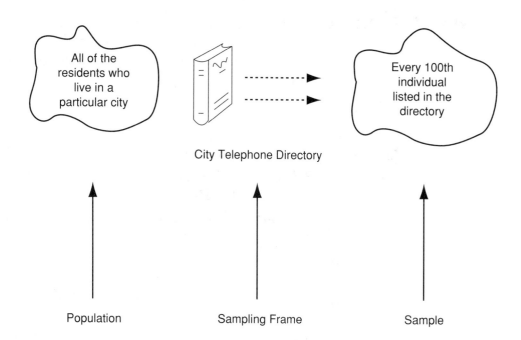

FIGURE 1.5   A SAMPLING FRAME

Variable

Description   A **variable** is any characteristic that can *vary,* or change, with respect to a group of people or objects of interest. The opposite of a variable is a **constant,** such as gender in a study involving only women.

Examples
- *Weight*—the weights of people vary, e.g., 110 lb, 140 lb, 195 lb.
- *Religion*—the religious preferences of people vary, e.g., Protestant, Catholic, Buddhist.
- *Occupation*—the occupations of people vary, e.g., architect, teacher, bus driver.
- *Grade point average*—the grade point averages of students vary, e.g., 2.5, 3.0, 3.5, 3.56.
- *Anxiety level*—this varies from quite low to very high in different individuals.
- *Psychological charactertics*—these include qualities such as self-confidence and authoritarianism, and vary in different people.

See also   Categorical variable; continuous variable; dependent/independent variable.

FIGURE 1.6   WHAT ARE THE VARIABLES HERE?

Constant

Description
The term **constant** in statistics refers to anything that does not change or vary. It is used in a number of ways: It is (a) a quantity that does not change in value in a particular situation, (b) a value that is the same for all units being analyzed or compared in an experiment or other study, or (c) the intercept and slope in a regression equation. The *intercept* is the point at which the regression line crosses the vertical axis. The *slope* is the degree of steepness of the regression line. Both are the same (i.e., constant) for all individuals represented in the regression.

Examples
- As an example of (a), in Indonesia, the price of a piece of art in a "fixed price" shop is not subject to bargaining, while in many shops, bargaining is expected.
- As an example of (b), consider a market researcher investigating men's attitudes toward the new features on several of this year's automobiles; gender would be a constant (only males are being interviewed).
- As an example of (c), the values of a and b in the regression equation $Y' = a + bX$ are the constants in that equation. a = the intercept and b = the slope.

See also   Intercept; regression equation; variable.

Social Security Numbers

062–23–2565

062–14–1983

062–61–0538

062–41–1569

062–33–1139

The number 062 is a constant in this set of numbers. It identifies the state in which the individual lived when he or she applied for a Social Security number.

FIGURE 1.7   A CONSTANT IN SOCIAL SECURITY NUMBERS

Statistic/Parameter

Description A **statistic** is a number that describes some characteristic of (i.e., the "status" of) a sample. It may or may not make use of all of the information in the sample that pertains to the characteristic. For example, suppose that all 1500 of the entering freshmen students at a private college are required to take the Graduate Record Examination (GRE). Suppose further that the 50 students who receive the highest scores on the GRE are then selected to be interviewed. The mean (arithmetic average) of the GRE scores of all 50 students would be a statistic. A statistic is very often used in connection with random sampling from some defined population, but this is not always the case. It may also be used with nonrandom samples, such as purposive or convenience samples.

It is helpful to distinguish between the concept of statistic and that of parameter. A *parameter* is an indicator of some characteristic of a population. That is, a parameter is the *true* value of the characteristic for the total group, or collection of objects (e.g., the 1500 freshmen mention above), from which one or more samples may be drawn. Note that if a numerical value is merely an *estimate,* based on sample data, of the population characteristic, it is a statistic, *not* a parameter.

Statistics are usually abbreviated or symbolized by English (Roman) letters. Parameters, on the other hand, are usually abbreviated by Greek letters.

Examples
- Examples of *statistics* include measures of central tendency, such as medians, modes, and means; measures of spread, such as ranges and standard deviations; and measures of relationships, such as correlation coefficients. Note, however, that they are based on sample data only, *not* on the population.

- Examples of *parameters* also include means, standard deviations, correlation coefficients, etc., but they refer to the entire population, not just to one or more samples selected from a population. The mean (average) score for the entire population of 1500 entering freshmen would be a parameter.

See also Population/sample.

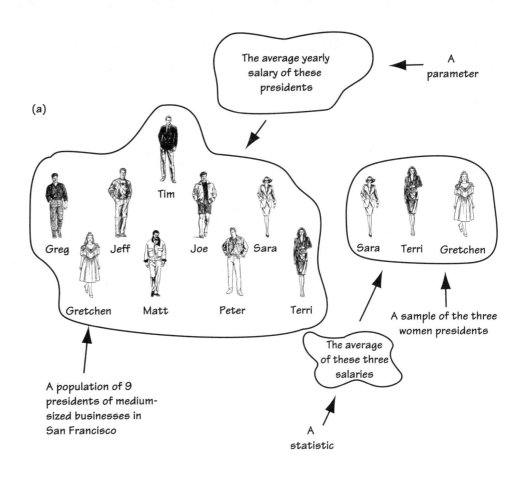

(a)

The average yearly salary of these presidents

A parameter

Tim

Greg Jeff Joe Sara

Gretchen Matt Peter Terri

Sara Terri Gretchen

A sample of the three women presidents

The average of these three salaries

A statistic

A population of 9 presidents of medium-sized businesses in San Francisco

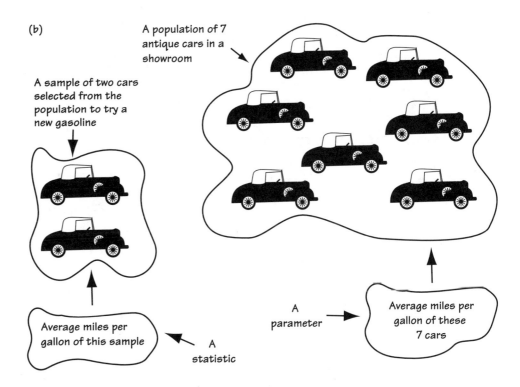

(b)

A population of 7 antique cars in a showroom

A sample of two cars selected from the population to try a new gasoline

Average miles per gallon of this sample

A statistic

A parameter

Average miles per gallon of these 7 cars

FIGURE 1.8 STATISTICS AND PARAMETERS

Margin of Error

Description
The **margin of error** says how closely the results of a sample correspond to how the population would respond if all its members had actually been surveyed. Newspapers and magazines regularly conduct sample surveys of a few thousand people to find out how they feel about various topics of interest. When properly conducted, such surveys are accurate to within a few percentage points, plus or minus. These few percentage points represent the margin of error.

Examples
- A researcher surveys a sample of 1000 people concerning their feelings about the President's recent speech on affirmative action. The results of the survey indicate that 65% of those surveyed agree with his views, with a margin of error of plus or minus three percentage points. This means that it is very likely that between 62% and 68% of the entire population agree with the President's views.

- A micrometer for measuring thickness is accurate to 1/100th of an inch. If the measurement obtained for a strip of metal is 0.15 inch, the true measurement can be expected to be between 0.14 and 0.16 inch. The margin for error is 0.01 inch.

See also Confidence interval.

FIGURE 1.9 MARGIN OF ERROR

Descriptive Statistics

Description The term **descriptive statistics** refers to a variety of methods that are used to simplify, summarize, organize, and identify relationships among quantitative data and sometimes to visually display such data. No attempt is made to draw inferences or conclusions about individuals other than those on whom the data were actually collected. Descriptive statistics are often contrasted with inferential statistics, whose methods are used to make *inferences* about a population, based on information about a sample drawn from that population.

Examples

- A professor gives a midterm examination in medieval history to a class of 22 students. After scoring the exams, he arranges the scores into the frequency distribution shown in Table 1.1. He then calculates the *mode* (the most frequent score) and the *mean* (the arithmetic average) of the scores in the distribution. Both the mode and the mean are descriptive statistics.

- A market researcher surveys a large randomly selected sample of people in an Eastern city concerning their breakfast preferences. She finds the percentages shown in the pie chart in Figure 1.10. These percentages are descriptive statistics.

See also Inferential statistics; mean; standard deviation.

TABLE 1.1 Frequency Distribution of Scores on a Midterm Exam in Medieval History (100 Points Possible)

Score	Frequency
97	1
96	2
93	1
89	3
87	4
84	2
80	2
75	5
70	2
	$n = 22$

Descriptive Statistics

Sum of scores = 1840
Mean = 83.64
Mode = 75

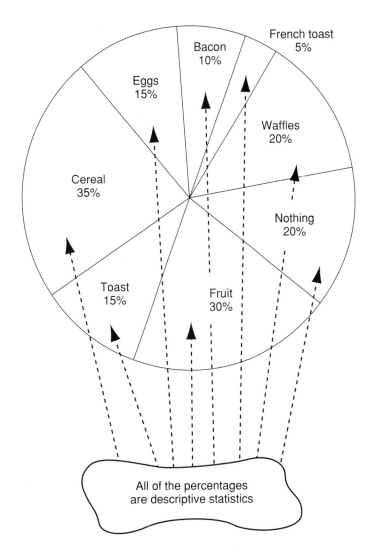

FIGURE 1.10 PIE CHART SHOWING DIFFERENT BREAKFAST PREFERENCES EXPRESSED IN PERCENTS

Inferential Statistics

Description   **Inferential statistics** are statistics that help one to make inferences or draw conclusions about a population or about how likely it is that a result could have been obtained by chance, on the basis of information obtained from a sample.

Examples
- A polling organization surveys a random sample of 1500 adults about their attitudes toward their City Council's performance during the past year. The survey results reveal that 55% approve of the Council's performance, 35% disapprove, and 10% have no opinion. The organization then states (infers) that these percentages indicate how the entire city feels about the Council's performance. Inferential statistics help us to decide how legitimate this inference is.

- The owner of a company that manufactures flashlight bulbs conducts a study on a random sample of 100 bulbs for a particular voltage to estimate the average life of bulbs in the collection of bulbs from which the sample was taken. The average length of time that the 100 bulbs stayed lit = 14.68 hours. Inferential statistics methods can now be used to indicate the approximate level of accuracy of the 14.68-hour average obtained on the sample.

See also   Descriptive statistics.

FIGURE 1.11 WHAT PERCENT APPROVE?

Representative Sample

Description A **representative sample** is one that is very similar (ideally, identical) in its characteristics to the population from which it was selected. When a sample is representative, one can make inferences from it about its population. The most effective way to obtain a representative sample is by *random sampling*.

Example Imagine that a researcher wants to survey a sample of union members to draw conclusions about their opinions on issues facing the union. The researcher would have more confidence that any inferences drawn about the members of the union as a whole were true if the sample strongly represented the population. If 70% of all the members are male and 30% are individuals who are over 50 years of age, the researcher could look at the sample to see whether there is a close match between the sample and these known population parameters. If the match is close, the researcher can more confidently come to conclusions about the entire union membership—more confidently, at any rate, than she could if the sample was, say, 80% male and 20% individuals over 50 years of age. In that case, the sample would *not* be representative; it would be *biased* because it would overrepresent males and underrepresent older workers.

See also Bias; convenience sample; purposive sample; random sampling.

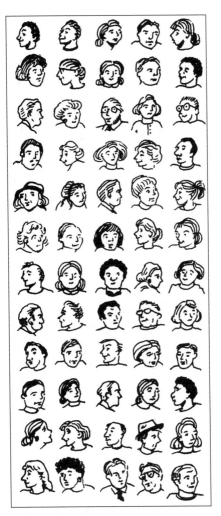

A Population of 60 Men and Women

A *nonrepresentative* sample (*n* = 12)
(2 women and 10 men)

A *representative* sample (*n* = 12)
(6 women and 6 men)

FIGURE 1.12 REPRESENTATIVE VERSUS NONREPRESENTA-
TIVE SAMPLES

Random Sampling

Description   **Random sampling** involves selecting a group of subjects (a **sample**) from a larger group (a population) so that each individual (or other unit of analysis) is chosen entirely by chance. When used without qualification, random sampling means "simple random sampling." Random sampling is also sometimes called "equal probability sampling" because every member of the population has an equal probability of being selected for inclusion in the sample. Note that a random sample is not the same thing as a haphazard or accidental sample. Using random sampling reduces the likelihood of a sample being biased. The best way to select a random sample is to use a **table of random numbers** found in most statistics texts.

Example   Ms. Jones wishes to interview a small group of people living in a retirement home as to how they feel about the quality of meals they are served. There are 100 men and women living in the home. Jones assigns a number from 0 to 99 to each of these individuals. This is the population about which she wishes to draw her conclusions. Jones uses a table of random numbers to select 10 of these individuals. She now has a random sample of 10 people she can interview about the meals served in the home.*

See also   Cluster random sample; convenience sample; population/ sample; purposive sample; stratified random sample; table of random numbers.

Note: Samples this small, even if randomly selected, are not recommended. We use a sample of 10 here to illustrate the idea of random sampling.

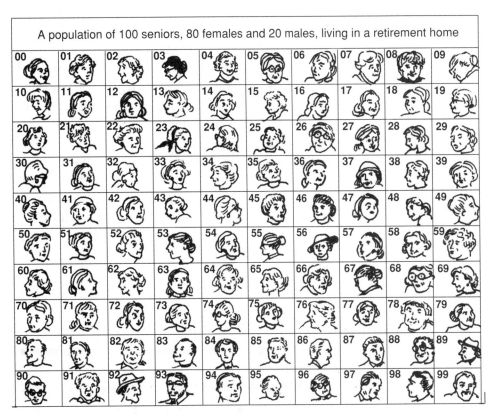

A population of 100 seniors, 80 females and 20 males, living in a retirement home

Researcher wishes to interview ten of the individuals in the population shown above. She assigns a different number, as shown, to each individual. She then uses a table of random numbers to select the ten individuals to be interviewed.

An example of one possible sample she might have selected, had she used this line

Sample A

Excerpt from a
Table of Random Numbers

7160	9321	6409	8321	2933
0411	5622	8691	3301	6518
9913	5117	6321	4567	9800
3216	5468	9761	0030	1246
8151	9839	0215	8790	2596

Note that sample Ⓐ consists of 8 women and 2 men. A different sample might contain a different proportion of men and women. For example, consider sample Ⓓ containing an equal number of men and women, which would have been selected had the researcher used the last line shown in the table.

Sample B

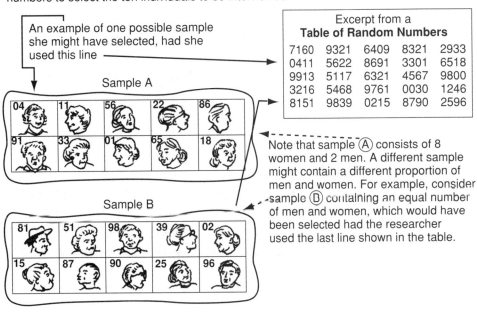

FIGURE 1.13 SELECTING A RANDOM SAMPLE

Table of Random Numbers

Description   A **table of random numbers** is a sequence of numbers arranged in such a way that the occurrence of any number in the sequence is no indication of the next number in the sequence. In the long run, all of the numbers in the table occur equally often. Rigorous methods are available on computers for checking the tables to make sure that the numbers actually do occur an equal number of times. Tables of random numbers, found in most statistics and many research textbooks, are used to select random samples or assign students randomly. Random number tables can be used starting with any page, any row, and any column. Ideally, the page, row, and column should be decided on before looking at the table. Computers can also be used to generate collections of random numbers.

Example   **TABLE 1.2**   A Table of Random Numbers

Line							
101	60940	72024	17868	24943	61790	90656	87964
102	18883	36009	19365	15412	39638	85453	46816
103	83485	41979	38448	48789	18338	24697	12230
104	07511	97150	21558	33586	54303	09547	27611
105	18804	47343	98112	28713	91111	11321	43444
106	55892	57157	13303	27831	92379	14567	44451
107	03316	39871	84443	16809	33479	05432	87690
108	32338	23579	56780	13245	66678	90000	00987
109	44575	35432	65321	54876	86548	97643	45612
110	62221	47169	45477	32768	17698	23890	87698
111	87174	54789	16234	12778	35467	37654	76598
112	10221	67809	32678	88900	76980	44567	88943
113	99232	11333	78001	43218	23434	56780	41109
114	00229	23665	34330	35790	21447	65478	86699
115	67800	11199	87002	13576	76789	76509	03412

See also   Population/sample; random sampling; unit.

I'd like to interview the owners of coffee shops () in San Francisco to find out what kind of coffee is most often purchased in their shop. But I don't have time to interview all of them--there are too many!

How many?

975! But I want to get a representative sample. Any ideas?

Sure. Use a table of random numbers to draw a random sample from the population of 975. Let me show you how.
- First, number all the coffee shops from 001 to 975.
- Then, begin at any line on the table, and read consecutively. Part of such a table is shown below. Let's use line 101:

Line

101	609	407	202	417	868	249	436	179	090	656	879	64
102	188	833	600	919	365	154	123	963	885	453	468	16
103	834	854	197	938	448	487	891	833	824	697	122	30

The first ten coffee shops in your sample would be those numbered:

609, 407, 202, 417, 868, 249, 436, 179, 90, & 656. Ten would be too few to ensure that your sample is truly representative, but I hope you get the idea!

FIGURE 1.14 HOW TO USE A TABLE OF RANDOM NUMBERS

Cluster Random Sample

Description **Cluster random sampling** is a method of sampling that involves drawing a random sample of *groups* rather than individuals from a population. It is frequently used when researchers are unable to get a complete list of the members of the population they wish to study but *are* able to get a list of groups (or "clusters") within the population. It is also used when obtaining a random sample would produce a list of subjects so widely scattered (20 in one state and 30 in another, for example) that the expense of obtaining data would be prohibitive.

The disadvantage of cluster sampling is that the initial selection of groups rather than individuals increases the likelihood of *sampling error*. The margin of error is therefore larger in cluster sampling than it is in simple or stratified random sampling. An advantage of cluster sampling is that it is usually much cheaper to do.

Examples
- A researcher who wishes to survey high school students to get their opinions as to how their schooling might be improved obtains a complete list of all the 90 high schools in the state (which are "clusters" of students). He then selects (using a table of random numbers) a sample of 20 high schools and surveys all of the students in these schools.

- The principal of a large urban high school divides her faculty of 90 teachers into groups ("clusters") according to the subjects they teach (algebra, U.S. history, PE, home economics, biology, etc.) and then randomly identifies all of the teachers in three randomly selected clusters to attend an educational conference.

See also Convenience sample; population/sample; purposive sample; random sampling; sampling error; stratified random sample; unit.

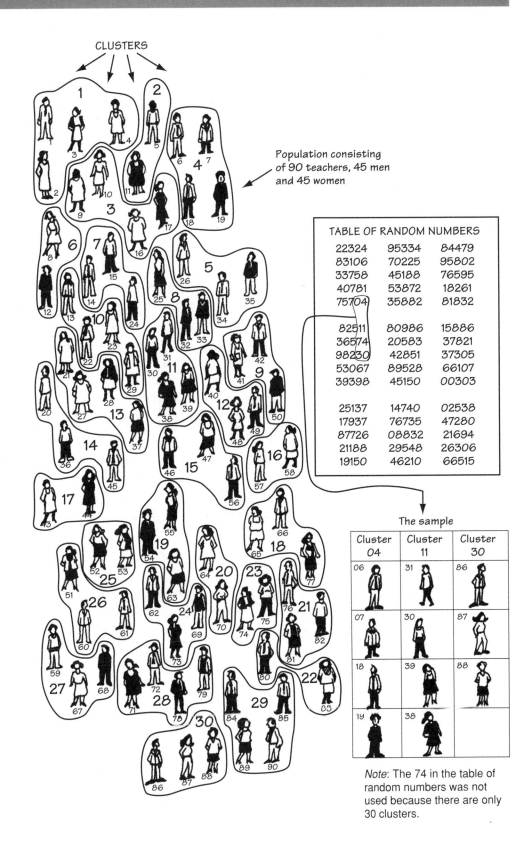

CLUSTERS

Population consisting
of 90 teachers, 45 men
and 45 women

TABLE OF RANDOM NUMBERS

22324	95334	84479
83106	70225	95802
33758	45188	76595
40781	53872	18261
75704	35882	81832
82511	80986	15886
36574	20583	37821
98230	42851	37305
53067	89528	66107
39398	45150	00303
25137	14740	02538
17937	76735	47280
87726	08832	21694
21188	29548	26306
19150	46210	66515

The sample

Cluster 04	Cluster 11	Cluster 30
06	31	86
07	30	87
18	39	88
19	38	

Note: The 74 in the table of
random numbers was not
used because there are only
30 clusters.

FIGURE 1.15 CLUSTER SAMPLING

Stratified Random Sample

Description   **Stratified random samples** are samples drawn randomly from particular categories (or "strata") of the population being studied. The purpose is to ensure that the sample is as much like the population as possible on the stratified variable(s) by making sure that each stratum is represented in the same proportion in both population and sample. It is particularly useful when the sample size is small.

Examples
- A researcher studying the effects of a drug with leukemia patients wants to be sure that the sample does not differ from the population with respect to age—a variable that is likely to affect the effectiveness of the drug. Since the assessment process is complex and unpleasant, a large random sample is not feasible. Therefore, a stratified random sample is selected. He determines that the sample will have the same percent in each age bracket (e.g., ages 10 to 19) as the population.
- A large bin of 1000 vegetables shown in Figure 1.16 is offered to a food distribution center at a very low price. The grower states that he would like to supply the center on a regular basis. Accordingly, the staff of the center decides to select a stratified sample of 40 vegetables to assess the quality of each type of vegetable in the bin.

See also   Cluster random sample; convenience sample; population/sample; purposive sample; random sampling; systematic sample; unit.

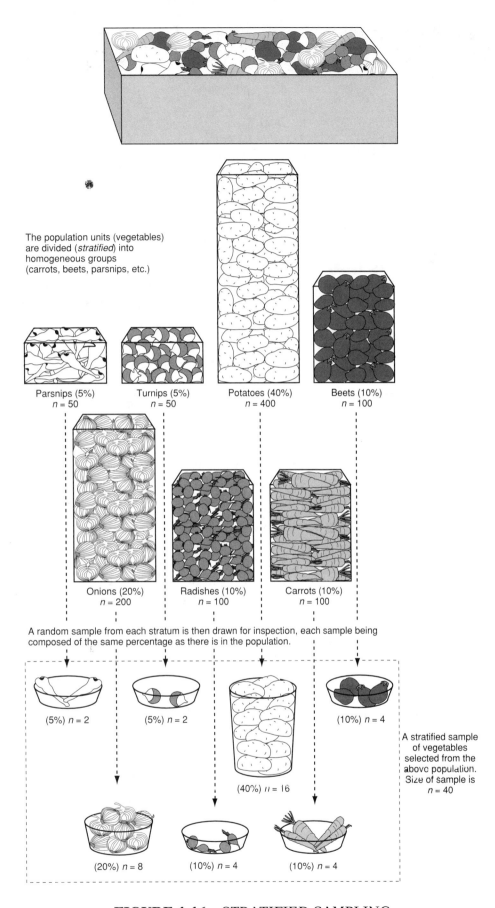

The population units (vegetables) are divided (*stratified*) into homogeneous groups (carrots, beets, parsnips, etc.)

Parsnips (5%) $n = 50$

Turnips (5%) $n = 50$

Potatoes (40%) $n = 400$

Beets (10%) $n = 100$

Onions (20%) $n = 200$

Radishes (10%) $n = 100$

Carrots (10%) $n = 100$

A random sample from each stratum is then drawn for inspection, each sample being composed of the same percentage as there is in the population.

(5%) $n = 2$

(5%) $n = 2$

(10%) $n = 4$

(40%) $n = 16$

A stratified sample of vegetables selected from the above population. Size of sample is $n = 40$

(20%) $n = 8$

(10%) $n = 4$

(10%) $n = 4$

FIGURE 1.16   STRATIFIED SAMPLING

Convenience Sample

Description A **convenience sample** is a group of subjects selected not because they are representative of a specified population, but merely because they are (conveniently) available.

Examples
- A news reporter for a local radio station asks passersby on a downtown street corner whether they favor or oppose building a new baseball stadium in the downtown area.
- A college professor interviews her own students concerning their feelings about a new textbook her department decided to use during the past semester.
- The manager of a local bookstore interviews the first 25 individuals who enter the store every Monday for a month to get their opinions about what kinds of books he should stock in the store.
- A researcher wants to study the attitudes of professional baseball players regarding a proposed baseball strike, so he interviews some of the players on his hometown team.
- A specialist in research design plans to conduct an exploratory *pilot study* on the preferences of research psychologists regarding different kinds of research designs. He decides to distribute a questionnaire to all of the research psychologists attending a local convention of psychologists.
- A telephone survey includes only those respondents who were home on the first call.

See also Cluster random sampling; purposive sample; random sample; representative sample; systematic sample.

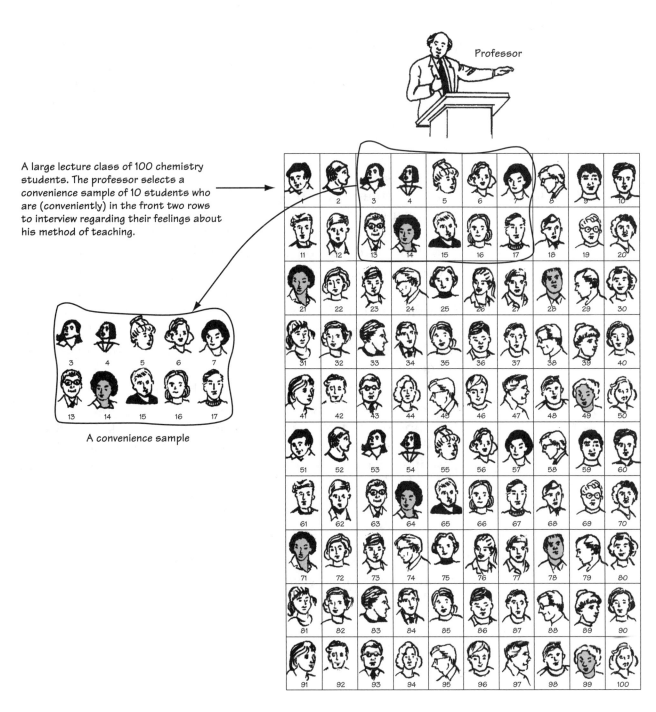

A large lecture class of 100 chemistry students. The professor selects a convenience sample of 10 students who are (conveniently) in the front two rows to interview regarding their feelings about his method of teaching.

Professor

A convenience sample

FIGURE 1.17   A CONVENIENCE SAMPLE

Purposive Sample

Description   A **purposive sample** is a sample composed of individuals selected deliberately (*on purpose*) because they are thought to be representative of the population or because they are thought to possess desired information about the population. This is generally a questionable thing to do, because the judgment that such samples are representative may be incorrect.

Examples
- An elementary school physical education teacher chooses the boy and girl in her class whom she feels can best represent the views of the other students as to the kinds of exercises she should include as a regular part of class activity.
- A researcher is asked to identify the unofficial power hierarchy in a large factory located in a midwestern city. He decides to interview the shop foreman, the union representative, and the worker identified by others as being "in the know" because he has been told they are the people who possess the information he needs.
- A sample of 10 social workers who have the most experience working with at-risk youths are selected from a population of 90 who are attending a professional meeting. These individuals are chosen because it is thought they are most likely to represent accurately the views of all social workers who work with such youths.

See also   Cluster random sample; convenience sample; random sampling; representative sample; systematic sample.

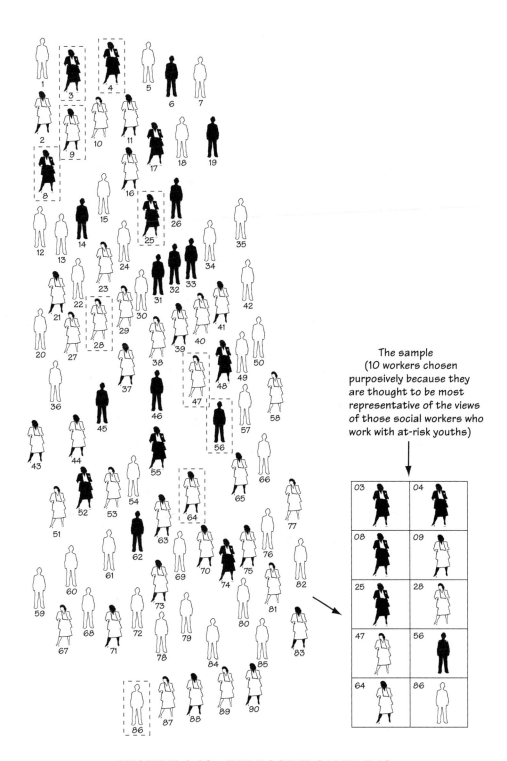

The sample (10 workers chosen purposively because they are thought to be most representative of the views of those social workers who work with at-risk youths)

FIGURE 1.18   PURPOSIVE SAMPLING

Systematic Sample

Description   A **systematic sample** is a sample that is obtained by taking every nth (e.g., every fifth or every seventh) subject or case from a list containing the total population. The size of the n is determined by dividing the population size by the desired sample size.

Examples
- Suppose a market researcher in a large city wants to draw a systematic sample of 1000 individuals from the city telephone directory, which contains 100,000 names. She would divide 100,000 by 1000 and get 100. She would therefore select every 100th name from the directory, starting with a randomly selected number between 1 and 100, say 39. She would select the 39th name on the list, the 139th, the 239th, and so forth.

- Traffic engineers in San Francisco who are conducting an automobile safety study might check the brakes and steering mechanisms of every 100th car exiting the toll booths on the Golden Gate Bridge.

- An inspector in a meat processing factory checks every 20th animal for damage.

- A quality control engineer in a pharmaceutical firm analyzes every 15th drug package for impurities.

See also   Cluster random sampling; convenience sample; purposive sample; random sample.

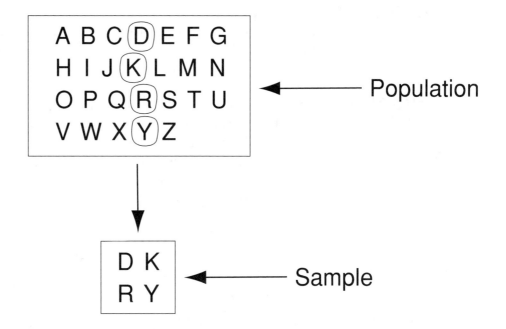

FIGURE 1.19   SYSTEMATIC SAMPLING

Multistage Sampling

Description **Multistage sampling** is a method of sampling that involves drawing a random sample from a population in two or more stages.

Example Suppose a market researcher wishes to test an advertisement designed for urban adults. One possibility would be to take a nationwide simple random sample of a few thousand adults selected from large cities. This would not be as easy as it sounds, however. First, one would need a list of all adults. There is no such list. And even if one could draw a simple random sample, the people would be scattered all over the United States. The cost to interview them would be prohibitive.

Instead, a multistage sample could be used. For example, the researcher could initially identify all cities with populations over 100,000 people.

- *First stage.* A random sample of those cities would be selected. Interviews would be conducted only in these cities.
- *Second stage.* Each city would then be divided into wards, and then one or more wards would be selected—again randomly.
- *Third stage.* Each ward would then be divided into precincts, and then one or more precincts would be chosen at random.
- *Fourth stage.* Each precinct would then be divided into blocks, and one or more blocks would then be chosen at random.
- *Fifth stage.* Finally, households would be drawn at random from each selected block, and then an adult member from each household would be interviewed.

See also Cluster random sample; convenience sample; population/sample; purposive sample; random sampling; stratified random sample.

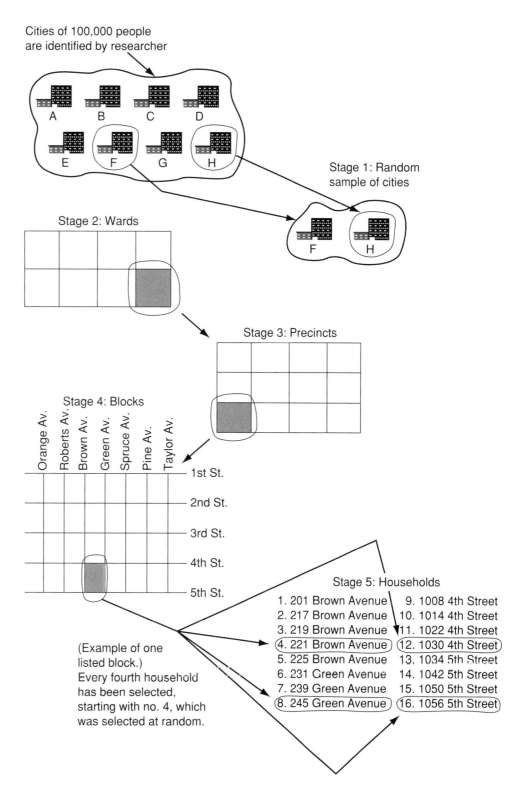

Cities of 100,000 people are identified by researcher

A B C D

E F G H

Stage 1: Random sample of cities

F H

Stage 2: Wards

Stage 3: Precincts

Stage 4: Blocks

Orange Av.
Roberts Av.
Brown Av.
Green Av.
Spruce Av.
Pine Av.
Taylor Av.

1st St.
2nd St.
3rd St.
4th St.
5th St.

(Example of one listed block.)
Every fourth household has been selected, starting with no. 4, which was selected at random.

Stage 5: Households

1. 201 Brown Avenue
2. 217 Brown Avenue
3. 219 Brown Avenue
4. 221 Brown Avenue
5. 225 Brown Avenue
6. 231 Green Avenue
7. 239 Green Avenue
8. 245 Green Avenue
9. 1008 4th Street
10. 1014 4th Street
11. 1022 4th Street
12. 1030 4th Street
13. 1034 5th Street
14. 1042 5th Street
15. 1050 5th Street
16. 1056 5th Street

FIGURE 1.20 MULTISTAGE SAMPLING

Sampling Distribution

Description A **sampling distribution** is a distribution of a particular statistic obtained (in theory) by selecting an infinite number of samples of a specific size from a population. Because statistics (e.g., means) are obtained from samples, a distribution of statistics is referred to as a sampling distribution.

Consider the mean. A sampling distribution of means is constructed by assuming that an infinite number of random samples of a particular size (n) were obtained from a population. Then the mean is computed from the scores of each of these samples, and then this group of means is arranged into a frequency distribution. We now have a distribution of sample means. Note that this distribution is *not* a distribution of scores, but rather one of *means*. Thus, the distribution of sample means is an example of a sampling distribution. Carrying this out in practice is usually impossible, but fortunately, sampling distributions have been derived mathematically for not only the mean, but also many other statistics. They are essential to the determination of *statistical significance*.

Example It can be shown mathematically that if the sample size is more than 30, the literal sampling described above would result in a distribution of means that takes the shape of the normal distribution having its own mean (mean of all the means) equal to the mean of the population from which the samples were drawn. Many, but not all, sampling distributions take the "normal" form.

A distribution of sample means is an example of a sampling distribution. In fact, it is often called the sampling distribution of the mean.

See also Frequency distribution; normal distribution; population/sample.

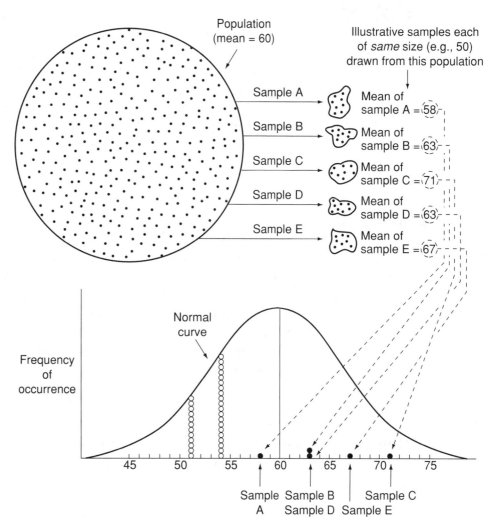

In this illustration, five samples have been selected, and the mean of each sample has been calculated. This procedure is (in theory) continued until an infinite number of samples is selected and their means calculated. The five means for samples A–E are shown. Each possible mean value would have a frequency (e.g., as shown for the values of 51 and 54). When all the means are plotted, the resulting smoothed frequency polygon will have the shape of a normal curve. This is known as the sampling distribution of the mean.

FIGURE 1.21 A SAMPLING DISTRIBUTION (OF MEANS)

Sampling Error

Description   **Samples** are seldom identical to the **population** from which they are selected with regard to any particular characteristic. The resulting difference between a sample value (i.e., a *statistic*) and its population value (i.e., a *parameter*) is known as sampling error. Furthermore, two samples selected from the same population are almost never exactly the same. They are composed of different individuals who possess different characteristics, score differently on a test (or other measure), and so on.

Example   Consider the population of adult women in the United States. We could select literally thousands of different samples of the same size from this population. Suppose we selected several samples with 50 women in each sample and determined their height. What do you think would be our chances of finding exactly the same mean (i.e., average) height in all of these samples? Very, very unlikely. Although any one of them *might* equal the mean of the entire population, this would be unlikely. These differences from the population mean are known as sampling error.

See also   Inferential statistics; population/sample; random sampling; standard error; standard error of estimate.

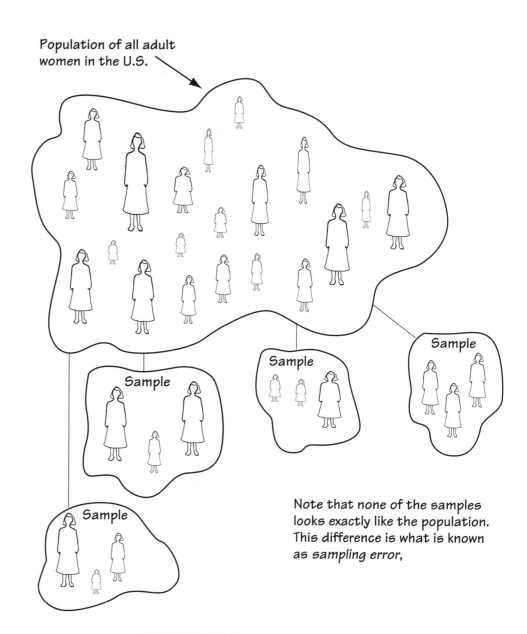

Population of all adult women in the U.S.

Sample

Sample

Sample

Sample

Note that none of the samples looks exactly like the population. This difference is what is known as sampling error,

FIGURE 1.22 SAMPLING ERROR

Sampling with and without Replacement

Description When drawing a sample from a population, one can either put (replace) or not put those drawn back into the population after each draw. Many statistical procedures assume sampling with replacement. However, it often is not possible to replace subjects, and hence many samples in the social and behavioral sciences are drawn without replacement. When the population or sample is large, this is usually not a serious problem.

Example For our example, let's use a deck of 52 playing cards. If you were to draw (sample) cards one at a time from the deck, recording the suit of the card after each draw, you could either replace the card and reshuffle the deck after each draw or not replace it. It matters whether you do so or not. Here's why.

If you drew a heart on the first draw, replaced it, and reshuffled the deck, your chances of drawing a heart on your second draw would be the same as they were on your first draw (13 in 52, or 25%). But if you did not replace the card after the first draw, there would now be one fewer card in the deck (the heart you drew). This *reduces* your chances of drawing a heart on the second draw (to 12 out of 51, or 23.5%).

See also Inferential statistics; population/sample; random sampling.

Imagine a box containing five apples.
Two draws are made at random from this box.

Suppose the first draw is a "5".

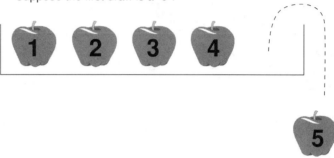

With replacement, the second draw is from:

Without replacement, the second draw is from:

FIGURE 1.23 SAMPLING WITH AND WITHOUT REPLACEMENT

ORGANIZING AND SUMMARIZING DATA

PART II

Set 2

The information that scientists and other researchers collect by various means must be clearly presented if we are to make any sense out of it. Information can be described and presented in a number of ways—in tables, in graphs and charts, and in words. In this section, we describe and illustrate some of the more important concepts involved in the presentation and description of information.

Tables, Graphs, and Distributions

Concepts in This Set

Listed Sequentially

frequency distribution
grouped frequency distribution
cumulative frequency distribution
percentile/percentile rank
pie chart
dot chart
bar graph
histogram
frequency polygon
stemplot
time series
normal distribution
skewed distribution
kurtosis

Listed Alphabetically

bar graph
cumulative frequency distribution
dot chart
frequency distribution
frequency polygon
grouped frequency distribution
histogram
kurtosis
normal distribution
percentile/percentile rank
pie chart
skewed distribution
stemplot
time series

Frequency Distribution

Description   A **frequency distribution** is a way of presenting data (e.g., scores on a test) that shows the number of cases that have each of the values of a particular variable, thus making it easier to see any patterns that exist in the data. It is a tally of the number of times each score appears in a group of scores.

Frequency distributions are often organized into two-column tables. The left-hand column contains a listing of all possible scores. The scores are arranged in order of size, usually with the highest scores at the top of the table and the lowest at the bottom. Each entry in the right-hand (or frequency) column indicates the number of individuals who received the score listed in each row of the left-hand column. The sum of the entries in the right-hand column is usually recorded at the bottom of the column and represents the total number of scores listed in the table.

Example   A psychologist is interested in what effects a broken home has on the self-concept of children and youths of various ages. He obtains a random sample of 40 such individuals and interviews them at length. Their ages (not in any order) are as follows:

19, 8, 7, 17, 6, 15, 12, 8, 14, 17
5, 13, 14, 10, 20, 13, 17, 14, 8, 6
10, 16, 9, 7, 14, 8, 15, 10, 7, 14
15, 12, 18, 15, 16, 19, 13, 5, 19, 5

(Note that, with the scores in a mixed-up sequence such as this, it is hard to see any kind of pattern or distribution.) Before commencing the interviews, the psychologist prepares a frequency distribution of the children's and youth's ages. The youngest is 5, and the oldest is 20. The ages are listed from 5 to 20, inclusive, in numerical order in the left-hand column, with age 5 at the bottom and age 20 at the top. The completed distribution is shown in Table 2.1.

See also   Grouped frequency distribution.

TABLE 2.1   A Frequency Distribution Table with Ungrouped Data, Showing Ages of 40 Children from Broken Homes

Age	Frequency
20	1
19	3
18	1
17	3
16	2
15	4
14	5
13	3
12	2
11	0
10	3
9	1
8	4
7	3
6	2
5	3
Total	**40**

Grouped Frequency Distribution

Description **Grouped frequency distributions** are often necessary when a distribution has too wide a range to be practical for preparing a simple (ungrouped) frequency distribution. In an ungrouped frequency distribution, every possible individual score or other value in the entire range is listed. Thus, if there were, say, 50 values in the entire range, it would be very long and cumbersome to use. To simplify the presentation, therefore, a grouped frequency distribution, in which the entire range is divided into *class intervals*, can be prepared. Class intervals are convenient groupings of the data on a continuous variable to make the data easier to analyze. In short, the frequencies for the values falling within each interval are thus combined. If the interval size is 5, for example, the number of rows needed for the corresponding table will be much less than would be needed if all the values were not grouped.

Example Suppose the IQs of a group of 40 individuals, placed in order from lowest to highest, are as follows:

> 67, 80, 86, 89, 91, 93, 98, 99, 102, 103, 103, 106,
> 108, 110, 111, 112, 114, 115, 119, 123, 123, 123, 125,
> 125, 126, 129, 129, 130, 131, 131, 135, 137, 137,
> 138, 141, 143, 145, 145, 154, 157.

The scores range from 67 to 157, with a total of 91 possible score values ($157 - 67 + 1 = 91$). If these scores are placed into an ungrouped frequency distribution table, 91 rows would be needed. On the other hand, if a grouped frequency distribution table with class intervals of size 10 is prepared (see Table 2.2), only 10 rows are needed. This table is now more convenient to use and interpret, although there is a cost. By grouping the data, some information is lost. Notice that all class intervals must be the same size and that each interval contains all the scores that fall within that interval. The bottom class interval, for example, would include any of the 10 possible scores that fall within the interval 60–69 (i.e., 60, 61, 62, 63, 64, 65, 66, 67, 68, or 69).

See also Frequency distribution.

TABLE 2.2 A Grouped Frequency Distribution Table

IQ Score		Frequency
150–159		2
140–149		4
130–139		7
120–129		8
110–119		6
100–109		5
90–99		4
80–89		3
70–79		0
60–69		<u>1</u>
Sum of the frequencies (total number of individuals):		40

Note that the interval width of these class intervals is 10, not 9. At first, it may appear that the size of each interval is 9 (e.g., 70–79), but actually it is 10 (70, 71, 72, 73, 74, 75, 76, 77, 78, 79). The interval here is 69.5 to 79.5 since 70 is midway between 69.5 and 70.5, and 79 is midway between 78.5 and 79.5.

Cumulative Frequency Distribution

Description   A **cumulative frequency distribution** table has an added column for a cumulative listing of the frequencies opposite the appropriate score or class interval. It may or may not have a column in which the frequencies are listed *non*cumulatively. The bottom entry in the cumulative column lists the frequency just for the bottom score or class interval. Subsequent entries in the table list the *sum* of the frequencies for a particular score or class interval and all those scores or class intervals below it. Each entry is therefore the sum of the frequency for its score or class interval and all frequencies below it. The entry at the top of the cumulative column, if calculated correctly, will be the sum total of all of the frequencies, corresponding to the total number of individuals in the distribution.

Example   Table 2.3 shows the number of aggressive acts reported for a group of 73 boys of different ages in a youth guidance center, over a three-month period. It contains both a noncumulative and a cumulative frequency column.

See also   Frequency distribution.

TABLE 2.3   Number of Aggressive Acts Reported for a Group of 73 Boys at a Youth Guidance Center Over a Three-Month Period

Age	Frequency	Cumulative Frequency
18–19	12	73 (12 + 61)
16–17	20	61 (20 + 41)
14–15	14	41 (14 + 27)
12–13	11	27 (11 + 16)
10–11	9	16 (9 + 7)
8–9	5	7 (5 + 2)
6–7	2	2
TOTAL	**73**	

Percentile/Percentile Rank

Description A **percentile** is a point on a scale of scores or other measurements below which a given percent of the scores fall. The 65th percentile is the point in a distribution of scores below which 65% of the scores fall; the 40th percentile is the point below which 40 percent fall, and so forth. If a person's height in a group of people is at the 90th percentile, this means that he or she is taller than 90% of the other individuals in the group.

Percentiles are often confused with *percentile ranks*. Percentiles are *points*. A person's percentile rank, on the other hand, is a number that indicates *rank*. It tells what percentage of the individuals being measured fall at or below a particular score. Thus, if 15% of the students in a sample *score* at or below 50 on an exam, then the 15th percentile is a score of 50. A person who obtains a score of 50 has a percentile rank of 15. An easy way to distinguish between the two concepts is to remember this: With a percentile, you find the *point* below which the (desired) percentage (of individuals) falls; with a percentile rank, you find the percent of individuals who fall at or below the desired *score* (or other measurement).

Examples
- Julie Thomas is at the 93rd percentile (a score of 680) on the Graduate Record Examination. This means that 93% of the individuals who took the examination scored below her and only 7% scored above her.

- Ninety-five percent of all students who took the Graduate Record Exam with Julie Thomas received a score at or lower than 700. Angela Ismay scored 700 on the exam. She has a percentile rank of 95.

See also Appendix A-1; cumulative frequency distribution; frequency distribution; grouped frequency distribution.

Percentile ranks are easy to calculate. You simply add the number of students below a given score to the number at that score and divide by the total number in the group. Multiplying the result by 100 gives you the percentile rank. Table 2.4 presents the scores of a group of 25 students on a history examination, along with the percentile rank for each score.

TABLE 2.4   Hypothetical Example of Raw Scores and Percentile Ranks

Raw Score	f	Cumulative Frequency	Percentile Rank	
95	1	25	100	
93	1	24	96	
88	2	23	92	
85	3	21	84	
79	1	18	72	
75	4	17	68	
70	6	13	52	
65	2	7	28	
62	1	5	20	← $(1 + 4)/25 \times 100 = 20$
58	1	4	16	
54	2	3	12	
50	1	1	4	
	$n = 25$			

Pie Chart

Description   A **pie chart** looks like a pie. It is used to illustrate the proportions of a categorical variable. A circle is drawn with areas marked off by straight lines from the center to represent the proportion of total units in each category. Different areas (the "slices" of the pie) are usually shown in different colors or markings, accompanied by a legend indicating what each area represents. A percentage is often superimposed on each area to indicate the exact proportion that the slice represents.

Example   Each year the city administration of San Francisco (similar to the administration of most cities) prepares and distributes a chart that illustrates the sources of the city's revenue for that year. The amount of money the city expects to receive from property taxes, the state's income tax, utilities fees, funds from grants, various city services, etc. are listed, and illustrated, frequently by means of a pie chart. One example of such a chart is shown in Figure 2.1.

See also   Bar graph; categorical variable; frequency distribution.

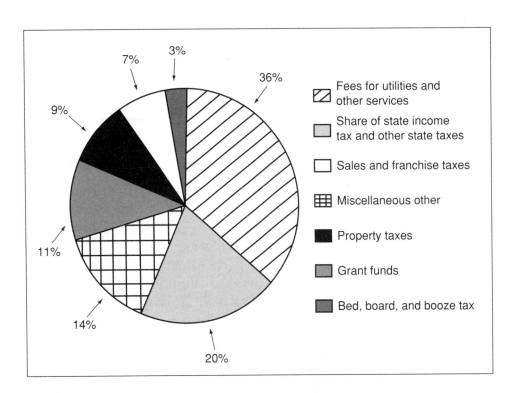

FIGURE 2.1 A PIE CHART SHOWING A CITY'S SOURCES OF REVENUE

Dot Chart

Description   A **dot chart** is a two-way graph that shows the percentages of a variable associated with different categories of the variable. The categories are usually indicated on the vertical axis and the number or percentage on the horizontal axis. A dotted line is drawn directly opposite each category, the length of the line indicating the percentage of the variable associated with that category.

Example   Suppose that the percentages for enrollment at various levels at a large university were as follows: freshmen, 25%; sophomores, 21%; juniors, 19%; seniors, 17%; master's degree candidates, 8%; doctoral candidates, 3%; and "other," 7%. Using a dot chart to show these percentages, we first list each category on the left side of the chart. We then draw a horizontal line of 25 dots opposite freshmen, a 21-dot line opposite sophomores, a 19-dot line opposite juniors, 17 dots opposite seniors, 8 dots opposite master's degree candidates, 3 dots opposite doctoral candidates, and 7 dots opposite "other," as shown in Figure 2.2.

See also   Frequency distribution; pie chart.

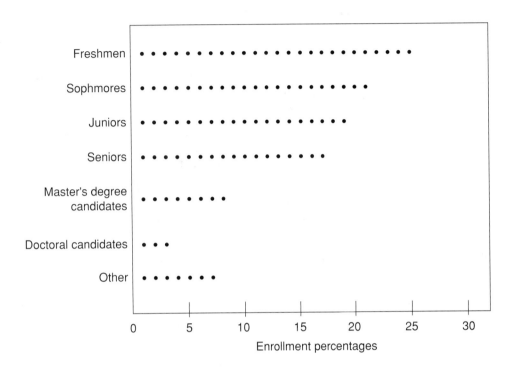

FIGURE 2.2 A DOT CHART SHOWING ENROLLMENT PERCENT-
AGES AT A UNIVERSITY

Bar Graph

Description A way to pictorially represent the frequency of occurrence within each category of a categorical variable, such as religious preference, class activities preferred by students, or ethnic group. Bars are drawn vertically from a horizontal baseline, along which the categories are listed. A vertical scale starting at 0 and increasing upward, placed at the extreme left side of the baseline, is used to indicate the frequency (or percentage) of occurrences in each of the listed categories. Because the data in a bar graph are categorical, the bars should not touch; in a histogram, which is used for interval or ratio data, they should touch.

Examples
- Example 1 in Figure 2.3 presents the average year-to-date returns in May of 1997 on popular mutual fund companies.
- Example 2 in Figure 2.3 presents the kinds of class activities preferred by a (hypothetical) class of high school juniors in U.S. history.

See also Categorical variable; frequency distribution; histogram; pie chart.

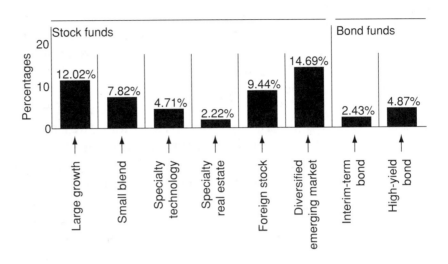

(a) Example 1: Average year-to-date
returns on popular mutual fund categories

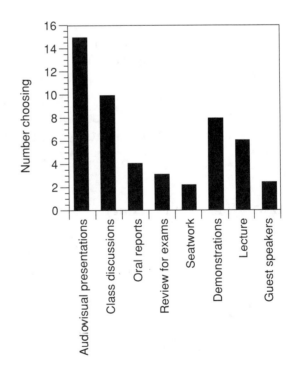

(b) Example 2: Class activities
preferred by a class of
11th-grade students

FIGURE 2.3 BAR GRAPHS

Histogram

Description   A **histogram** is a graph used to present interval or ratio data—that is, data measured on a continuous scale with equal intervals rather than in terms of categories or ranks. It is a way to make clearer the information contained in a frequency distribution. The frequencies of the various levels of the variable being illustrated are represented by the heights of bars. Sometimes the bars are shown horizontally; usually, they are drawn vertically, extending from a horizontal baseline (the horizontal axis), with numerical values increasing from left to right. Frequencies are shown on the vertical axis, starting at zero at the baseline and increasing upward. The height of each of the bars corresponds to the frequency of the interval that the bar represents. In contrast to bar graphs, histograms are drawn so that adjacent bars touch.

Example   Suppose that the ages of the members of a drama club ranged from 21 to 78 years. A histogram of their ages would be too wide if a bar were drawn for each member's age. This can be remedied by grouping the members' ages into class intervals of size 10 (21–30, 31–40, 41–50, 51–60, 61–70, and 71–80). A bar can then be drawn above each of these class intervals, resulting in six bars. The frequency for each class interval would then be shown by the height of its bar, representing the number of members whose age falls within the limits of that particular class interval.

See also   Bar graph; frequency distribution; *x-y* axes.

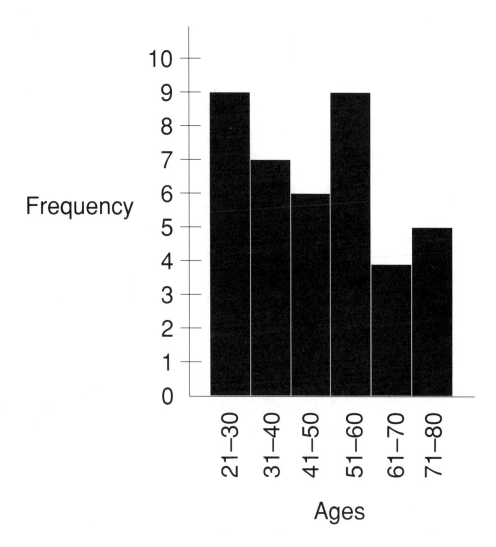

FIGURE 2.4   A HISTOGRAM SHOWING THE DISTRIBUTION OF AGES OF MEMBERS OF A DRAMA CLUB

Frequency Polygon

Description   **Frequency polygons,** like histograms, present the information contained in frequency distribution tables visually. They make it easy to see at a glance how the scores are distributed—if most of them are clustered near the middle, for example; if there are large gaps in the data; and so forth. Frequency polygons are drawn by using both the horizontal and vertical axes on a graph. The horizontal axis is labeled with the name of the characteristic being illustrated, along with a scale of numbers placed at equal intervals to indicate the various amounts or values of the characteristic. Frequencies are shown on the vertical axis, starting with zero at the horizontal axis. A dot is then placed directly above each characteristic at a height corresponding to its frequency, and the dots are joined with straight lines. Then, a line is drawn from the dot for the lowest score down to the left on the horizontal axis. A similar line is drawn from the dot for the highest score down to the right on the horizontal axis. This is called "anchoring" the polygon.

Example   To get a better picture of the distribution of ages of the 40 children from broken homes who are to be interviewed (see the frequency distribution in Table 2.1 on page 51), a psychologist arranges their ages into a frequency polygon.

See also   Frequency distribution; grouped frequency distribution; histogram; *x-y* axes.

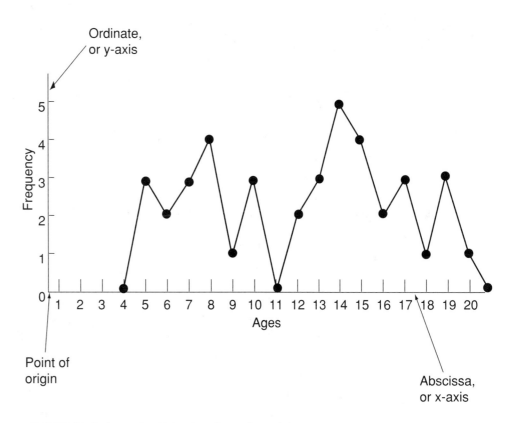

FIGURE 2.5   A FREQUENCY POLYGON SHOWING THE DISTRIBUTION OF AGES OF 40 CHILDREN FROM BROKEN HOMES

Stemplot

Description A **stemplot** is a graphic way of recording data that presents raw scores (numbers, etc.) in a visual, histogram-like display. Stemplots are particularly useful in recording small data sets. The main advantage of a stemplot over other forms of visual displays is that it not only presents a clear picture of the frequency distribution, but it also loses none of the original data. Stemplots are also sometimes called *stem-and-leaf displays*.

Example Listed below are the number of home runs that Babe Ruth hit during each of the years he played with the New York Yankees (1920–1934):

54, 59, 35, 41, 46, 25, 47, 60, 54, 46, 49, 46, 41, 34, 22

To make a stemplot, we use the first digit of the number as the *stem*. Write the stems vertically, lowest at the top, with a vertical line to their right. Then write the second digit of each number as the leaf, writing each leaf to the right of the proper stem. The first entry of 54, therefore, would show a 4 written opposite the stem 5. The second entry would show a 9 written to the right of the 4, again opposite the stem 5. The third entry would show a 5 written opposite the stem 3. The final step is then to arrange the leaves in order from left to right. Here are the three steps:

2			2	5 2		2	2 5
3			3	5 4		3	4 5
4			4	1 6 7 6 9 6 1		4	1 1 6 6 6 7 9
5			5	4 9 4		5	4 4 9
6			6	0		6	0

Step 1. The stems   Step 2. The leaves   Step 3. Order the leaves

See also Bar graph; histogram.

Home runs Hit by Babe Ruth 🏏 **,** 
1920–1934, while playing for the
New York Yankees

Stem	Leaves
2	2 5
3	4 5
4	1 1 6 6 6 7 9
5	4 4 9
6	0

A *back-to-back stemplot* comparing the
home runs hit by Ruth with those hit by
Roger Maris during his 10 years in the
major leagues (1956–1965). It shows clearly
that Ruth was the superior hitter.

Maris 		Ruth 
8	0	
6 4 3	1	
8 6 3	2	2 5
9 3	3	4 5
	4	1 1 6 6 6 7 9
	5	4 4 9
1	6	0

FIGURE 2.6   TWO STEMPLOTS SHOWING THE HOME RUNS HIT
BY BABE RUTH AND ROGER MARIS DURING THEIR MAJOR
LEAGUE CAREERS

Time Series

Description   A **time series** is a set of measurements of a single variable recorded at different times. Usually (although not always), the measurement takes place at regular intervals, such as monthly or yearly. Time series data are often shown by means of a time series plot.

Examples
- The annual amount of rainfall in San Francisco, California, from 1950 to the present.
- The monthly unemployment rate from January 1970 to December 1979.
- The average temperature in New York City each month for 20 years.
- The changes in the average weekly price of regular unleaded gasoline over the course of a year.
- The Dow-Jones daily averages for the past 12 months.
- The weekly spelling quiz scores of a group of third graders for a semester.

See also   Frequency polygon.

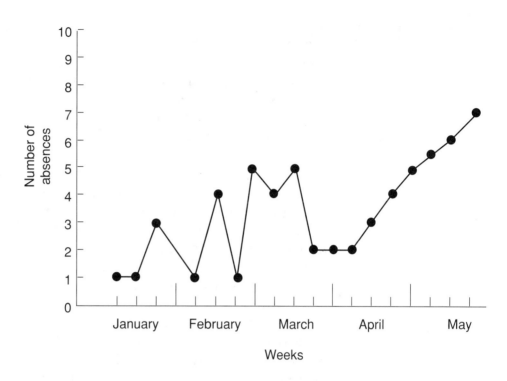

FIGURE 2.7 TIME SERIES PLOT: WEEKLY ABSENCES OF A CLASS OF THIRD GRADERS

Normal Distribution

Description Many frequency distributions of data tend to follow a certain shape called a *normal distribution*. When shown as a curve, it is one of many types of *distribution curves*. For a distribution curve, a smooth curving line is drawn instead of straight lines connecting dots, as in a frequency polygon. The result is a "smoothed out" polygon—a generalized distribution, or model, of scores that can represent a variety of sets of data. The curve for a normal distribution is often referred to as the *normal curve*.

When a distribution curve is normal, the large majority of scores (or other values) are concentrated in the middle of the distribution, and scores decrease in frequency the farther away from the middle they are. Extreme scores are relatively rare (have low frequencies). The exact shape for the normal curve is based on a precise mathematical equation, which relates each score or number (shown on the *x*-axis) to its frequency (shown on the *y*-axis). The normal curve is symmetrical and bell shaped. The total area under the normal curve represents 100% of the scores (or other values) in a normal distribution. In such a curve, the mean, median, and mode are identical, all falling at the exact center of the distribution. Since the curve is symmetrical, 50% of the scores are below the mean and 50% are above it. A normal distribution curve can be tall and narrow or wide and "squatty," depending on the size of units chosen for the baseline.

Example The distribution of some human characteristics, such as height and weight, are approximately normally distributed, while many human abilities, such as spatial ability, manual dexterity, creativity, and mental ability, are often assumed to be. Its theoretical properties make it basic to the use of inferential statistics.

See also Frequency distribution; frequency polygon; standard score; *x-y* axes.

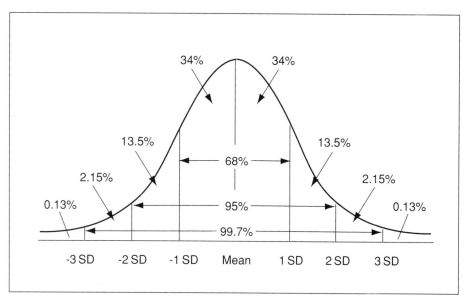

(a) Percentages under the normal curve

(b) A normal distribution—almost!

FIGURE 2.8 NORMAL DISTRIBUTIONS

Skewed Distribution

Description A **skewed distribution** is a distribution of scores or other measures that, when plotted on a graph, produces a nonsymmetrical curve. Skewed distributions have a large concentration of cases on one side of the distribution and a smaller number of more widely scattered cases on the other side.

A *positively skewed* distribution is one in which infrequent cases are near the high end of the scale, with the greater concentration of cases on the low end. It is skewed to the right. A *negatively skewed* distribution has the opposite pattern; the infrequent cases are near the low end, with the greater concentration of cases on the high end. It is skewed to the left.

Examples
- Imagine a school with a policy of not promoting students from the fourth to the fifth grade until they have achieved an 80% level of mastery of the objectives for the fourth grade. This is likely to mean that some of the slower-learning students would have to be in the fourth grade for two, three, or perhaps even more years. As a result, there would be a few fourth graders who would be older and taller than the typical age and height for that grade. Suppose that someone selected 20 fourth-grade boys in such a school and obtained a distribution of their heights in order of size. This distribution is shown in Table 2.5. Notice that the heaviest concentration of students' heights is at the low part of the scale, and the smaller number of more widely scattered individuals is in the high range. This is a positively skewed distribution.

- Imagine a 20-member baseball team of 8 to 11-year-old boys. When they play teams from other clubs, the coach selects the best players in order to have the best possible chance of winning. This means that the older boys are likely to play much more than the younger boys, because the older boys are usually taller and stronger and usually have more skill. The team's distribution in Table 2.6 shows the heights of the boys selected to play in one of the games. The relatively small number of younger boys in the low part of the distribution indicates that it is negatively skewed.

See also Frequency distribution; frequency polygon.

TABLE 2.5 Heights of Fourth Grade Boys

Height (in inches)	Frequency
47-49	🧑🧑🧑
50-52	🧑🧑🧑🧑🧑🧑
53-55	🧑🧑🧑🧑🧑🧑🧑
56-58	🧑
59-61	🧑🧑
62-64	
65-67	🧑

TABLE 2.6 Heights of Boys' Baseball Team

Height (in inches)	Frequency
51	🧑
52	
53	🧑
54	🧑🧑
55	🧑🧑🧑
56	🧑🧑🧑🧑🧑🧑🧑🧑
57	🧑🧑🧑🧑🧑

Kurtosis

Description **Kurtosis** is a measure of the flatness or peakedness of a (unimodal) frequency distribution. It indicates the extent to which a distribution departs from the normal (bell-shaped) curve. If a frequency distribution curve is flatter in shape than a normal bell-shaped curve, it is *platykurtic*. If it is more peaked, it is *leptokurtic*.

Examples
- An example of a platykurtic curve might be that showing the income in a town where there are a few very wealthy people and a few very poor people but most people have incomes in between these extremes.
- An example of a leptokurtic curve might be one showing the size of the trees in an area in which most of the trees were clearcut a few years earlier and replaced by a tree farm.
- An example of a probable change from a platykurtic distribution curve to a leptokurtic one is the tree diameter in a natural forest (with a more-or-less even age distribution) that was devastated by fire and then re-seeds. Some years later, most trees will be of similar size, with only a few larger or smaller.

See also Frequency distribution; frequency polygon; normal distribution.

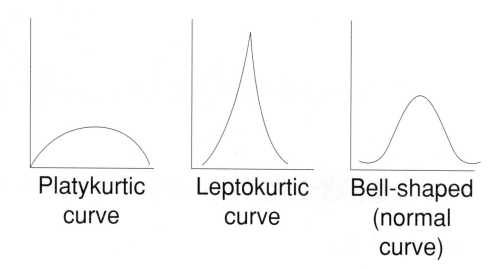

Platykurtic curve   Leptokurtic curve   Bell-shaped (normal curve)

FIGURE 2.9   EXAMPLES OF KURTOSIS

Set 3

Researchers usually collect so much data that they must, of necessity, condense it in some way. A long list of numbers by itself, for instance, is not very informative. To make sense out of data, it has to be not only organized (e.g., by means of a table or graph), but also summarized. There are three kinds of useful information about a set of data, each of which can be described and expressed in different ways. One useful concept is the *shape* of the data, which can be derived from various kinds of pictures of the data, as you saw in Set 2. A second useful concept is the idea of the *center* of the data. Where is it, and how do we locate it? A third useful concept is the *variability* of the data. How spread out are the data, and how do we determine this? In this section, therefore, we describe and illustrate some of the more important concepts involved in determining the center and spread of a set of data.

Centers and Spreads (Summary Measures)

Concepts in This Set

Listed Sequentially

mean
algorithm
weighted mean
median
mode
range
interquartile range
boxplot
variance
standard deviation
standard score
standardized normal distribution

Listed Alphabetically

algorithm
boxplot
interquartile range
mean
median
mode
range
standard deviation
standardized normal distribution
standard score
variance
weighted mean

Mean

Definition The **mean** is the arithmetic average of a set of scores. To calculate the mean, add up the values and divide by the total number of cases. In a *population*, the mean is often symbolized by μ (mu); in a sample, by $\bar{X}$ ("X-bar"). It is the statistic that is used the most frequently to indicate the middle point in a distribution of numerical values.

Examples
- Table 3.1 shows scores of 10 students on a 20-item test. The mean is the total value of all scores divided by the number of scores. Thus, 790/10 = 79.

- Means are computed on a wide range of variables, including the heights of individuals, household incomes, daily maximum temperatures in a city for an entire summer, annual repair costs reported by owners of a certain make and model of automobile, and salaries of professional wrestlers.

- The owner of a small dress shop wants to know the average number of dresses sold each month by the different salespersons she employs. Every day, she lists the number of dresses each person sells. At the end of the month, she adds up each person's daily sales, and then divides the total by the number of days in the month. The resulting number represents the average (the mean) number of dresses sold by each salesperson.

See also Median; mode.

TABLE 3.1 Distribution of 10 Scores on a Midterm

Student	Score on Midterm
Ann	97
Kim	96
Thomasine	87
Angelica	81
Jordan	80
Paul	80
Tara	80
Feliz	78
Alphonso	66
Larry	45
Total	790

Individual	Height (in inches)	Weight
Phil	71"	165 lb
Tom	68"	150 lb
Wendy	74"	170 lb
Anh	57"	90 lb
Tony	77"	240 lb
Victoria	67"	139 lb
Sum	414"	954 lb
Mean	**69"**	**159 lb**

414 divided by 6 = 69
954 divided by 6 = 159

The average (mean) height for these six individuals is 5'9".
Their average (mean) weight is 159 lb.

FIGURE 3.1 THE MEAN HEIGHT AND WEIGHT OF A GROUP OF SIX BUSINESSPEOPLE

Algorithm

Description An **algorithm** is a clearly specified set of steps or calculations to be followed in performing a task or solving a problem.

Examples
- How to prepare the perfect three-minute egg:
    Step 1: Bring at least three cups of water to a boil.
    Step 2: Carefully place the egg in the water.
    Step 3: Leave the egg in the water exactly three minutes.
    Step 4: Remove the egg, crack the eggshell, and place the contents on plate.
    Step 5: Add salt or Tabasco sauce to taste.
- How to calculate the mean of a distribution of scores:
    Step 1: Add up all the scores in a distribution of scores.
    Step 2: Divide the total by the number of scores (the formula is $\bar{x} = \dfrac{\Sigma x}{n}$).

    where $\bar{x}$ = mean,
    Σx = sum of all the scores in the distribution,
    n = number of scores in the distribution.

See also Mean; weighted mean; probability rules.

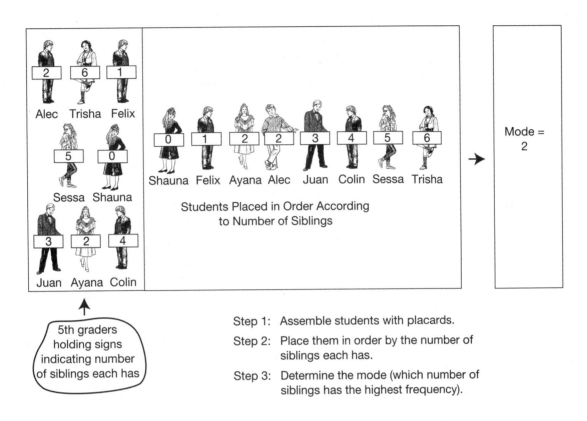

Step 1: Assemble students with placards.

Step 2: Place them in order by the number of siblings each has.

Step 3: Determine the mode (which number of siblings has the highest frequency).

FIGURE 3.2 HOW MANY SIBLINGS DO YOU HAVE?

Algorithm **83**

Weighted Mean

Description   It is sometimes necessary to compute the mean of two or more groups of different sizes by using the mean of each. Calculating the **weighted mean** takes the *size* of the groups into account. You simply multiply the mean of each group by the number of individuals in the group, add up the results, and divide by the total number of individuals in all of the groups. This is the grand (or overall) mean.

Example   Suppose that the individuals in four groups of people were asked what their weekly salary was. The number of individuals in each group and the mean salary of the group are shown in Table 3.2.

To calculate the grand (overall) mean salary for the four groups, you cannot just add up the means for each group and divide by four (this would give you an average salary of $546.00). There are so many more individuals in Group II that you have to give their mean more weight to get the true overall average. To do so, you multiply the mean for each group (column B) by the number of people in the group (column A), add up the results (column C), and divide by the total number of individuals in all four groups: $100,129/197 = $508.27.

TABLE 3.2   Mean Salaries of Four Groups of People

Group	(A) Number of individuals in group	(B) Mean Salary	(C) A × B
I	33	$498	16,434
II	100	$449	44,900
III	29	$750	21,750
IV	35	$487	17,045
Total	**197**	**$508.27**	**100,129**

↑
Weighted mean

See also   Mean.

FIGURE 3.3 WHEN A WEIGHTED MEAN IS CALLED FOR

Median

Description The **median** is one of several measures of central tendency—a kind of "average." It is the point that divides a distribution of numerical values in half so that there are the same number of values above this point as there are below it. It is the middle score in a set of ranked scores when there are an *uneven* number of scores in the distribution. When there are an *even* number of scores in the distribution, the median is found by taking an average of the two middle scores. Although the median has limitations for complex analyses, it should be used instead of the mean whenever a set of scores is highly skewed. In such cases, the mean can be misleading because of the weight given to a few extreme scores.

Examples
- Eleven students took a midterm examination in a high school chemistry course and received the following scores: 95, 90, 90, 89, 89, 87, 84, 70, 64, 53, 45. The median score is 87.

- Only 10 students took the second examination in the course (one had dropped the class); they received these scores: 93, 90, 90, 88, 86, 84, 84, 83, 82, 70. The median score in this case is 85.

- A first-grade teacher in an elementary school prepared the histogram shown in Table 3.3, consisting of the ages, in months, of the 34 boys and girls in her class. There are 18 boys altogether. The median age of this group of boys is the age for which the number of boys younger than this age is exactly equal to the number of boys older than this age. By counting nine boys up from the bottom, starting with 67 months, we reach 72 months, the *median age* of this group of boys.

  There are 16 girls altogether. Starting at the bottom, we find that there are eight girls aged 71 months or younger and eight girls 72 months or older. The median, therefore, is somewhere between 71 and 72 months. But where, exactly? We have now encountered some arbitrariness regarding medians. In this case, any age between 71.1 and 71.9 months could be reported as the median, because exactly half of the girls are younger than *any* of those ages, and half are older. This illustrates the fact that the median cannot always be precisely defined. The usual convention is simply to split the difference and say that the median is exactly halfway between the two middle values. In this case, therefore, we would report the *median* age for this group of girls to be 71.5 months.

See Also Mean; mode; skewed distribution.

TABLE 3.3 Median Age of a Group of 18 Boys and 16 Girls in an Elementary School

Age in Months	Boys	Girls
80	●	●
79		
78		●
77	●	
76		●
75	● ●	
74	●	●
73	● ●	●
median → 72	● ● ● ●	● ● ●
71	●	● ● ● ← median
70	● ● ●	● ●
69	● ●	●
68		
67	●	●
66		●
Total	(18)	(16)
Median	72	71.5

Mode

Description The **mode** is one of several measures of central tendency—a kind of "average." It is the category or numerical value that occurs most often in a set of data. If there are two categories or values considerably higher than the others, the data set is referred to as a *bimodal distribution*. If there are more than two, it is called a *multimodal distribution*.

Examples
■ Here are the scores of 18 students who took a 20-word spelling test:

12, 14, 15, 15, 15, 15, 16, 16, 16, 16, 16, 17, 17, 17, 18, 19, 19, 20

What is the mode in this distribution of scores? 16, because that is the score received by the largest number of students (see Figure 3.4a).

■ Forty people participating in a program at a senior citizen's center were asked which kind of fruit they liked best. The purpose of the question was to find out which fruits should be served at meals at the center, and how often. The number of choices for each kind of fruit are shown in Figure 3.4b. As you can see, the fruit that was named most often was apples. The category of apples, therefore, is the mode (note that the mode is *not* the number 9). That is all there is to determining the mode: Find the value or category that occurs the largest number of times.

See also Mean; median.

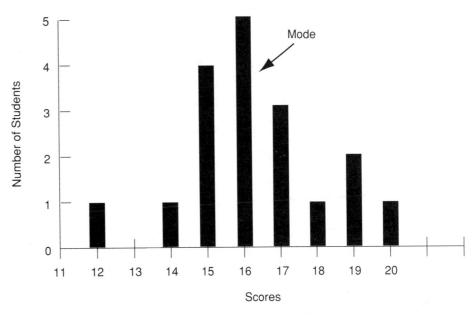

(a) Modal score of 18 students on a 20-word spelling test

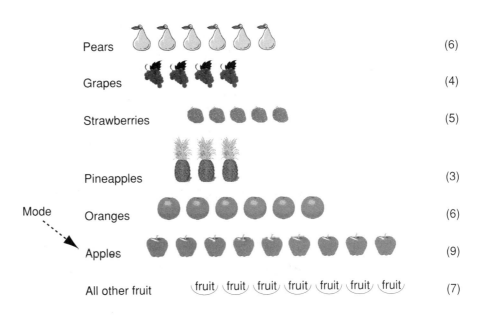

(b) Preferred Breakfast Fruits of a Group of Senior Citizens

FIGURE 3.4 THE MODE

Range

Description
The **range** is a measure of spread. It is not a highly precise one, however, because its computation involves only the one lowest and the one highest value in a distribution. One version of the range is computed by simply subtracting the lowest value from the highest. The resulting difference is the range. Another version is that the range is the difference between the highest and the lowest values *plus 1*. It is sometimes referred to as the *inclusive* range. Statisticians often prefer this method of computing the range. The reason can be seen in the example below.

Examples
- Suppose a teacher gave a test that turned out to be surprisingly easy for the students and that all of the scores were either 99 or 100. If the computations are done by the first method, the range is 100–99, which is 1. But there are *two scores;* it therefore makes more sense to say that the range is 2 (because the numbers range across the two scores of 99 and 100). Determining the inclusive range (100 – 99 + 1 = 2) assures us that the computed value for the range is the same as the maximum possible number of different numerical values that could be involved.

- As a second example, consider the following distribution of scores:

    20, 21, 21, 22, 22, 23, 23, 23, 24, 25, 25, 26

    The first version described above indicates that the range is (26 – 20), or 6. The inclusive range, however, gives us (26 – 20 + 1), or 7.

- Table 3.4 indicates the temperatures during the month of August in Omaha, Nebraska, in a typical year. Note that the coolest temperature was 72°; the hottest was 93°.

See also Interquartile range (IQR); standard deviation; variance.

TABLE 3.4 Typical Temperatures During the Month of August in Omaha, Nebraska

Temperature	Number of Days
93	2
92	0
91	3
90	7
89	2
88	0
87	1
86	5
85	0
84	1
83	0
82	1
81	1
80	0
79	1
78	1
77	0
76	1
75	1
74	2
73	0
72	2
Total Days = 31	

Range

High – Low = 93 – 72 = $\boxed{21}$

or

High – Low + 1 = 93 – 72 + 1 = $\boxed{22}$

Interquartile Range (IQR)

Description   The **interquartile range (IQR)** is a measure of dispersion or spread calculated by taking the difference between the first and third quartiles (i.e., the 25th and 75th percentiles) of a distribution. The first quartile (referred to as Q_1, or the 25th percentile) is the point in a distribution that separates the individuals with scores in the lowest one-fourth of the distribution from the other three-fourths. The third quartile (referred to as Q_3, or the 75th percentile) is the point in a distribution that separates the highest-scoring one-fourth of individuals from the lower-scoring three-fourths.

The interquartile range is a measure of the variability of scores or other measurements. Thus, the more widely scattered the scores in a distribution are, the larger is the difference expected between Q_1 and Q_3. When a distribution is skewed, researchers often report a *five-number summary*, consisting of the lowest score in the distribution, Q_1, the median (Q_2), Q_3, and the highest score. Boxplots often are drawn to illustrate such summaries. A variation is the *semi-interquartile range*, which is the interquartile range divided by 2.

Example   Suppose that the scores for 20 students on a statistics quiz were 7, 9, 12, 12, 14, 16, 17, 17, 19, 19, 21, 22, 23, 24, 24, 26, 28, 28, 29, and 30. Q_1 would be 15, the point separating the lowest one-fourth of the scores from the others. Q_3 would be 25, the point dividing the top one-fourth from the other three-fourths. The interquartile range, then, would be simply $Q_3 - Q_1$, which is (25 – 15), or 10.

See also   Boxplot; percentile/percentile rank.

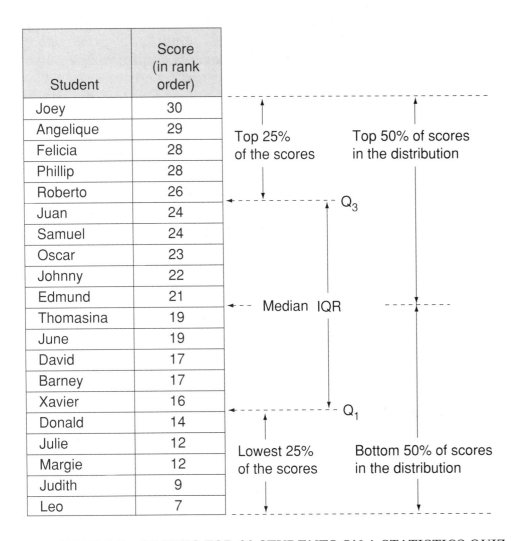

Student	Score (in rank order)
Joey	30
Angelique	29
Felicia	28
Phillip	28
Roberto	26
Juan	24
Samuel	24
Oscar	23
Johnny	22
Edmund	21
Thomasina	19
June	19
David	17
Barney	17
Xavier	16
Donald	14
Julie	12
Margie	12
Judith	9
Leo	7

Top 25% of the scores

Top 50% of scores in the distribution

Q_3

Median IQR

Q_1

Lowest 25% of the scores

Bottom 50% of scores in the distribution

FIGURE 3.5   SCORES FOR 20 STUDENTS ON A STATISTICS QUIZ

Boxplot

Description   A **boxplot** is a type of graph in which boxes and lines are drawn to show the shape, center, and spread of a frequency distribution. Boxplots are especially helpful in comparing two or more distributions and illustrating whether or not a distribution is *skewed* and contains *outliers*. It is sometimes called a "box-and-whiskers" diagram.

The upper and lower boundaries of the box are drawn at the 25th and 75th *percentiles*. Thus, the box represents the interquartile range (IQR)—the middle 50% of the values in the distribution. Frequencies are shown on the vertical axis; the name of the box (or boxes) is shown on the horizontal axis.

A horizontal line is drawn in the middle of the box opposite the *median* of the distribution.

Two lines are drawn extending from the box (sometimes called the "whiskers").

Any values beyond the ends of the whiskers are considered *outliers* (if they are more than 1.5 IQR's from the end of the box) and are sometimes marked with an "O."

Example   Suppose that a medical researcher wishes to compare the number of face-lifts performed during a given year by a group of male and female doctors. Here are the numbers performed by each group:

> Group I: Male doctors (*n* = 15): 20, 25, 25, **27**, 28, 31, 33, **34**, 36, 37, 44, **50**, 59, 85, 86
> Group II: Female doctors (*n* = 15): 5, 6, 7, **10**, 14, 17, 18, **19**, 25, 29, 31, **33**, 35, 35, 40

The median for Group I is 34, the upper quartile is 50, and the lower quartile is 27. The median for Group II is 19, the upper quartile is 33, and the lower quartile is 10. The highest number in Group I is 86; the lowest is 20. The highest number in Group II is 40; the lowest is 5. Boxplots were drawn by using the procedure described above.

See also   Frequency distribution; interquartile range (IQR); median; outlier; percentile/percentile rank; range.

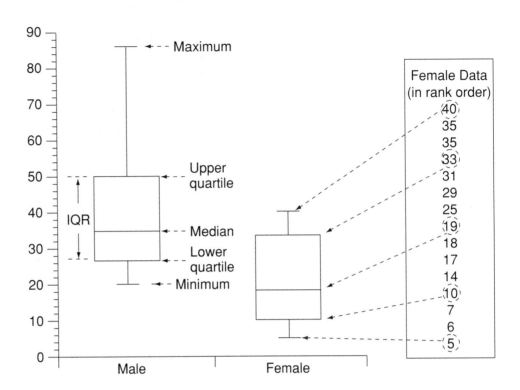

FIGURE 3.6 BOXPLOT COMPARING THE NUMBER OF FACE-LIFTS PERFORMED BY 15 MALE AND 15 FEMALE PHYSICIANS

Variance

Description   **Variance** is a measure of the spread of scores in a distribution of scores, that is, how far they are spread out or dispersed. It is the square of the standard deviation. The smaller the variance, the closer the individual cases are to the mean, and vice versa.

     Specifically, the variance of a population is the mean of the sum of the squared deviations (the sum of squares, or SS) from the mean. The variance of a sample is calculated by dividing the SS by the number in the sample. Taking the square root of the variance gives one the standard deviation.

Example   To improve a rather dismal free-throw-shooting record at the start of the season, the members of a high school boys' basketball team practice diligently. As a result, the average number of free throws completed during games by the team improves. The number completed early in the season ranges from 0 to 7, whereas the number completed late in the season ranges from 5 to 9. The early season variance was 6.00. By comparison, the variance late in the season was 2.00 (see Table 3.5).

See also   Interquartile range; mean; range; standard deviation.

TABLE 3.5 A Comparison of the Average Number of Free Throws Made per Game Early and Late in the Season by Five Players on a High School Basketball Team

	Early in the Season				Late in the Season		
Player's Number	Number of Baskets	Score Minus Mean	Score Minus Mean (Squared)	Player's Number	Number of Baskets	Score Minus Mean	Score Minus Mean (Squared)
(4)	0	−3	9	(4)	5	−2	4
(11)	3	0	0	(11)	7	0	0
(18)	7	+4	16	(18)	9	+2	4
(22)	1	−2	4	(22)	8	+1	1
(27)	4	+1	1	(27)	6	−1	1
Totals→	15	0	30	Totals→	35	0	10
	(Mean = 3)				(Mean = 7)		

$$\text{Early in season variance} = \frac{\text{SS}}{n} \frac{(-3)^2 + (0)^2 + (4)^2 + (-2)^2 + (1)^2}{5} = \frac{30}{5} = 6.00$$

$$\text{Late in season variance} = \frac{\text{SS}}{n} \frac{(-2)^2 + (0)^2 + (2)^2 + (+1)^2 + (-1)^2}{5} = \frac{10}{5} = 2.00$$

Note that the team members improve considerably in their shooting later in the season, becoming much more consistent. Hence the variability (the *variance*) of the team's shooting ability *decreases* accordingly.

Standard Deviation

Description

The **standard deviation** is a statistic that shows the spread, or dispersion of scores in a distribution of scores or other measurements. It is the most widely used and accepted measure of variability. It tells us *how much*, on the average, the values in a numerical distribution deviate from the mean. The more widely the scores are spread out, the larger is the standard deviation. The standard deviation is calculated by taking the square root of the *variance*. It is symbolized usually by SD, *s*, or σ.

Examples

- Suppose the students in two college biology classes took the same examination. In the first class, the students' scores on the test range from 70 to 86; in the second, the scores range from 65 to 95. The standard deviation would be larger for the scores of the second class than the first.

- Consider the weights of professional football players. These men typically weigh between about 200 pounds and well over 300 pounds. Compare their weights with the weights of men in the general population—in which some men weigh less than 100 pounds and a few weigh over 500 pounds. Which group would you expect to have the larger standard deviation: the football players or the men in the general population? The answer is the men in the general population. Note that we are not after the typical or average weight; we are interested in the amount of *dispersion*, or "scatter," among the weights. There is much more variability among the weights of men in the general population—from those who are slightly built to those who are heavily built—than among the weights of men on a professional football team. Such a team is a relatively *homogeneous* group of near-giants. The deviations of individual weights from the mean for the football players would be relatively small, so the standard deviation would be relatively small.

- The players on a boys' basketball team and a men's basketball team stand side by side. The boys' heights range from 4'6" to 5'9". The men's heights range from 6'0" to 6'7". The heights of the boys differ (that is, they *vary*) more than do the heights of the men. Note that this is true even though all of the boys are shorter than any of the men. In other words, there is a greater spread or dispersion of heights among the boys than there is among the men. The standard deviation for the boys' team, accordingly, is higher than that for the men's team. The computed standard deviation for the boys' heights is 5.25 inches; for the men, it is 2.45 inches.

See also Interquartile range; range; variance.

FIGURE 3.7 STANDARD DEVIATIONS FOR BOYS' AND MEN'S BASKETBALL TEAMS

Standard Score

Description   A **standard score** is a measure of relative or comparative standing in a group. Standard scores are arrived at by transforming raw scores so that one can compare scores in different distributions. The most basic form of standard score is the *z-score*. In a distribution of *z*-scores, the mean is 0 and the standard deviation is 1. Thus, a *z*-score of 1.5 is one and one-half standard deviations above the mean. A *z*-score of –2.0 is two standard deviations below the mean, and so forth. *z*-scores are especially useful for comparing the performance of different individuals on different measures, each with a different mean and standard deviation.

Example   Amy Adams wants to compare her scores on the midterm examinations she took in physics, biology, and chemistry. She is a bit perplexed as to how to do this, however, since each of the exams had a different number of questions and they varied in difficulty. What can she do?

Amy can convert her scores on each of the exams to standard scores. The higher her standard score on each exam, the better she did in comparison with the other students who took that exam. The highest standard score would then indicate the exam on which she did the best (see Table 3.6). Amy scored one standard deviation above the mean on the physics exam, 1.5 standard deviations above the mean on her biology examination, but one standard deviation *below* the mean on her chemistry examination. Thus, even though her *raw score* was lower on the biology exam, the conversion to standard scores shows that she actually did better, in comparison with the other students taking the exam, in biology than in physics or chemistry.

See also   Frequency distribution; mean; normal distribution; standard deviation.

TABLE 3.6   Amy's Midterm Exam Scores in Three Subjects

	Physics	Biology	Chemistry
Amy's Scores	90	85	93
Mean	85	82	94
Standard deviation	5	2	1
z-score	+1	+1.5	−1

FIGURE 3.8   STANDARD SCORES

Standardized Normal Distribution

Description Researchers often standardize a set of scores to make them easier to understand. A standardized score simply represents the number of standard deviations an observed value or score falls from the mean. A **standardized normal distribution** is a distribution of scores that has been converted into a distribution of z-scores with a mean of 0 and a standard deviation of 1. Sometimes, however, other numbers are substituted in place of 0 and 1, as in the following example.

Example IQ scores, as measured by the Stanford-Binet IQ test, are one example of a standardized normal distribution. Scores from the Stanford-Binet have a normal distribution with a mean of 100 and a standard deviation of 16. A person who received a score of 116 on this test would have an IQ that is exactly one standard deviation above the mean of 100. We can say, therefore, that this individual has a *standardized score* of 1. Someone with an IQ of 84 would have a standardized score of –1, since he or she would be exactly one standard deviation below the mean.

See also Frequency distribution; normal distribution; standard score.

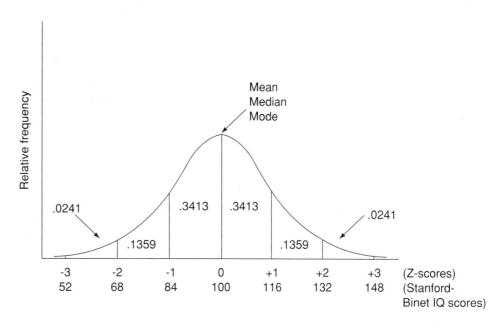

FIGURE 3.9 A STANDARDIZED NORMAL DISTRIBUTION

Set 4

Data can be collected in many ways. Before we obtain data from the respondents in a survey, or the subjects in an experiment, or on biological diversity in a forest, for example, we have to know how to measure whichever characteristics are of interest to us. To do so, we need to assign numbers to these characteristics. The assignment of numbers to represent the characteristics of a person or object, in fact, is what measurement is all about. In this section, we describe and illustrate several of the more important concepts involved in the process of measurement.

Measurement

Concepts in This Set

Listed Sequentially

data
measurement
percentage/proportion
rates versus counts
ratio
Likert scale
index number
bias
halo effect
ceiling effect
reliability
reliability coefficient
standard error of measurement
validity
norm
nominal scale
ordinal scale
interval scale
ratio scale

Listed Alphabetically

bias
ceiling effect
data
halo effect
index number
interval scale
Likert scale
measurement
nominal scale
norm
ordinal scale
percentage/proportion
rates versus counts
ratio
ratio scale
reliability
reliability coefficient
standard error of measurement
validity

Data

Description **Data** are collections of information obtained from observations, records, and other sources. ("Data" is the plural; the singular is "datum," but usage varies.) Data are the raw material on which statistical operations are performed. They are often collections of scores or other measurements obtained during a number of observations. Data are often thought of as being quantitative, but they can also take other forms, such as eyewitness reports, audio recordings of interviews, or videotapes of actual events.

Examples
- The number of accidents of each kind at a dangerous intersection as reported in police records
- Answers people give to questions asked of them in an interview
- The number of correct answers on an examination
- How many thought questions a teacher asks as recorded by an observer on videotape
- Prices listed for the same garment in different stores
- Baseball records showing how often players hit, walked, struck out, and flied out during a season
- Stock prices as quoted in newspapers
- The number of children living in a particular neighborhood
- The number of single-parent families listed in the U.S. Census report

See also Statistic.

Some real data obtained as part of a classroom experiment: 90 San Francisco State students reported their weight, with these results:

Males: 140 145 170 190 155 106 150 190 195 132 140 141 153 145 170 163 175 170 180 135 170 157 105 185 200 155 180 155 215 150 145 163 155 150 155 150 180 160 135 160 130 155 150 148 155 150 140 180 190 145 150 164 140 142 136

Females: 140 120 130 138 121 125 116 145 150 112 125 130 120 130 123 119 118 116 135 125 118 122 115 98 115 150 111 116 87 90 125 133 110 150 107

FIGURE 4.1 WEIGHTS AS DATA

Measurement

Description   To **measure** a characteristic or property of a person or object is to assign a number to represent the characteristic or property. An *instrument* of some sort is usually used to make the measurement.

Examples
- To measure the width of a table or the length of a sofa, we use a tape measure (that's the instrument). The measurement most likely would be in inches.

- To measure how fast an athlete can run a mile, we use a stopwatch (that's the instrument). The measurement would be in minutes and seconds.

- To measure something that is quite abstract (and rather hard to define), such as "self-esteem," researchers often ask respondents to read a set of statements and then indicate the degree to which they agree with the statements. For example, a questionnaire designed to measure self-esteem might ask people to indicate their level of agreement, from "strongly agree" to "strongly disagree," with statements such as "I generally have a high opinion of myself" or "I feel quite capable of being able to perform most tasks with which I am confronted." In this case, the questionnaire is the instrument. The measurement would be a score indicating how the individuals respond to the questions.

See also   Reliability; validity.

(a) How fast can you run a mile?

(b) Where do you stand?

FIGURE 4.2 EXAMPLES OF MEASUREMENT

Percentage/Proportion

Description   A **proportion** is a number between 0 and 100 that is calculated by dividing the number of items having a certain characteristic by the total number of items. If you multiply a proportion by 100, you get a **percentage.**

Examples
- If a parking lot contains 480 automobiles and 120 of these are Chevrolets, the proportion of Chevrolets would be (120/480), or .25. Twenty-five percent (.25 × 100 = 25%) of the automobiles in the lot would be Chevrolets.
- Table 4.1 shows the percentage and proportions of different kinds of majors among students in a university graduating class.

See also   Cumulative frequency distribution; dot chart; index number; percentile/percentile rank; pie chart; rates vs. counts.

TABLE 4.1 Proportion/Percentage of Different Kinds of Majors in a University Graduating Class

Major	Number	Proportion	Percentage
Business	630	.30	30
Social science	105	.05	5
Education	462	.22	22
Physical science	63	.03	3
English	525	.25	25
Physical education	252	.12	12
Mathematics	63	.03	3
Total	**2100**	**1.00**	**100**

Rates versus Counts

Description   A **rate** is the *proportion* or *percentage* of times that something occurs. A **count** is simply the number of times a thing occurs.

Example   Suppose that customers returned 40 sweaters to Brown's Fashion Shoppe but that only 20 sweaters were returned to Green's Boutique. Brown's Fashion Shoppe sold 200 sweaters, but Green's sold only 50. Which shop had the most satisfied customers (at least judging by sweater returns)?

The *count* is 40 sweaters returned to Brown's, and 20 sweaters returned to Green's. The *rate,* however, is 40/200, which equals .20 or 20% to Brown's, compared to 20/50, which equals .40, or 40% to Green's. A greater *proportion* of customers returned their sweater purchases to Green's Boutique, even though the *number* (count) of sweaters returned to Brown's Fashion Shoppe was higher. The level of customer satisfaction, therefore, was higher at Brown's (assuming that returning a sweater indicates that the customer was not satisfied with it).

See also   Frequency distribution; percentage/proportion.

FIGURE 4.3 RATE VERSUS COUNT

Ratio

Description A **ratio** shows the relationship between two numbers; it is expressed as a fraction or by simply separating the two numbers with a colon. Thus, the ratio of three dogs to four cats in a household (3/4 or 3:4) indicates the relative proportion of each type of pet.

Examples

- Suppose that a parking lot attendant counted the number of different makes of automobiles parked in the lot where she works on Saturday afternoons. If on a particular Saturday, 40 Toyotas and 10 Chevrolets were parked in the lot, the ratio of Toyotas to Chevrolets would be 40/10, or 40:10, or 4:1, or 4 to 1.

- The number of men who voted at a polling place in the last city election was 319 and the number of women was 237. The ratio of the number of women to the number of men is computed by dividing 237 by 319, which equals .7429, or approximately 74/100.

See also Percentage/proportion.

FIGURE 4.4 RATIO OF VANS TO CARS IN A CITY PARKING LOT

Likert Scale

Description   The **Likert scale** is a widely used scale in which respondents are given a list of statements and asked to indicate whether they "strongly agree," "agree," are "undecided," "disagree," or "strongly disagree." Likert scales are widely used, are comparatively easy to construct, are often used to measure attitudes, and usually have high reliability coefficients.

Examples
- A professor of education who directs the teacher training program at a state college wants to find out what students think about various issues related to empowering classroom teachers in elementary and secondary schools. She therefore decides to prepare a list of statements (a Likert scale) that will ask students to indicate their opinions on various aspects of this issue. A few of the items in the scale she designed are shown in Figure 4.5.
- Other variables sometimes measured by Likert scales include attitudes of students toward school subjects (e.g., mathematics); beliefs regarding the necessity of changing certain government policies; the level of employee satisfaction with their job; and opinions regarding various policy changes by the management of a large apartment complex.

See also   Interval scale; ordinal scale.

Instructions: Circle the choice after each statement that indicates your opinion.

1. All professors of education should be required to spend at least six months teaching at the elementary or secondary level every five years.

Strongly agree	Agree	Undecided	Disagree	Strongly disagree
(5)	(4)	(3)	(2)	(1)

2. Teachers' unions should be abolished.

Strongly agree	Agree	Undecided	Disagree	Strongly disagree
(5)	(4)	(3)	(2)	(1)

3. All school administrators should be required by law to teach at least one class in a public school classroom every year.

Strongly agree	Agree	Undecided	Disagree	Strongly disagree
(5)	(4)	(3)	(2)	(1)

FIGURE 4.5   EXAMPLES OF ITEMS FROM A LIKERT SCALE MEASURING ATTITUDE TOWARD TEACHER EMPOWERMENT

Index Number

Description An **index number** provides a comparison of costs or other variables at two or more points in time, usually in percentage terms. A common example is how the cost of something at one time compares to its cost at another time. The most common indicator of change in the cost of living is the *Consumer Price Index* (CPI), published by the U.S. Bureau of Labor Statistics. The CPI is supposed to measure changes in the cost of a "market basket" of goods and services that a typical consumer would be likely to purchase. The cost of this collection of goods and services is measured during a certain period of time (called the "base period") and then again at subsequent intervals. At any given time, the CPI is simply a comparison of what things cost currently with what they cost during the base period.

Examples
- If it cost you \$325 to rent a particular apartment in 1985 but \$475 for the same unit in 1996, then the price index would be $\left(\dfrac{475}{325}\right) \times 100 = 146\%$. In other words, to rent this apartment in 1996 cost 146% of what it cost to rent in 1985. We could also say that the cost of renting this apartment increased by 46%.

- It cost \$4.50 to see a movie in 1985. In 1997, it cost \$7.00. The movie price index would be $\left(\dfrac{7.00}{4.50}\right) \times 100 = 156\%$. Or we could say that movie prices increased by 56% during this period.

See also Percentage/proportion.

TABLE 4.2 Yearly Increase in Costs of Attending a Small Private College

Year	Tuition	Room and Board	Books	Total	College Index Number
1st year (freshman)	$4,000	$6,000	$700	$10,700	100 (base period)
2nd year (sophomore)	$4,400	$6,500	$750	$11,650	$(11,650/10,700) \times 100 = 109$
3rd year (junior)	$4,900	$7,000	$800	$12,700	$(12,700/10,700) \times 100 = 119$
4th year (senior)	$5,500	$7,600	$900	$14,000	$(14,000/10,700) \times 100 = 131$

FIGURE 4.6 CAN YOU BELIEVE THE PRICE OF BREAD?

Bias

Description   **Bias** is anything that produces consistent error(s) in the presentation of data. It is a systematic mistake or prejudice in one direction.

Examples
- If a bathroom scale is incorrectly adjusted by the manufacturer and is therefore always a few pounds over, individuals who weigh themselves will get a biased view of their own weight.

- Sometimes, if a survey is conducted to obtain support for a particular cause, the survey questions can be deliberately worded in a biased way. Suppose, for example, that a pro-school-prayer group and an anti-school-prayer group wanted to conduct surveys to get the best possible show of support for their respective positions. Here are two questions that are almost certain to produce different responses:

    1. Would you agree that prayer in schools, as an example of religious freedom, should be permitted?
    2. Would you agree that prayer in schools takes valuable instructional time and thus should not be permitted?

- The amount of crime occurring in the United States can be measured by counting the number of crimes reported by victims to local police departments or by surveying a random sample of households throughout the nation. The FBI publishes police reports, while the National Crime Victimization survey publishes data obtained by the survey. The victim survey supposedly shows more than twice as many crimes as the FBI report. Why? Because people are more likely to indicate that a crime has been committed when replying to a survey than to make a police report. Which do you think is biased?

See also   Ceiling effect; extraneous variable; halo effect; Hawthorne effect; purposive sample; validity.

(a) A Biased Bathroom Scale

(b) A Biased Impression

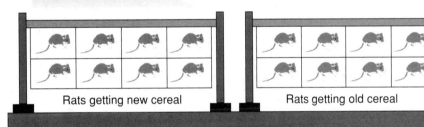

Rats getting new cereal   Rats getting old cereal

A researcher wants to study the nutritional effects of a new cereal product. She compares the weight gains of rats fed the new cereal and rats fed the old cereal. All the rats that receive the new cereal are housed where they get more exercise and sunlight than the rats getting the old cereal. Unwittingly, the researcher has *biased* the outcome in favor of the new cereal.

(c) Biasing the Results of an Experiment

FIGURE 4.7 EXAMPLES OF BIAS

Halo Effect

Description The **halo effect** is the tendency of judges to rate something higher than is warranted because of prior positive experiences with that being rated (e.g., people, performances, objects, or events).

Examples

- Suppose a skater has won two previous competitions that a particular judge has scored. In a third competition, the skater does not skate as well as she did in her previous performances. However, she might receive a higher rating than she really deserves because of the halo effect of her earlier accomplishments.

- One of the best players on a high school tennis team is close to losing his eligibility to play because of low grades. In grading his papers, some of his teachers may hesitate to give him a low mark because this would weaken the team's chances of winning the league championship.

- The personnel director for a large company believes that men are more effective in managerial positions than women. As a result, he tends to be more favorably impressed by men's resumes than women's.

- A frequent complaint of professional basketball players is that, because of a history of winning, some teams end a game with a fewer number of fouls called by officials than is justified.

See also Bias; extraneous variable.

FIGURE 4.8 A HALO EFFECT

Ceiling Effect

Description The **ceiling effect** is what happens when many of the individuals in a study score at or very near the possible upper limit of measurement (i.e., the "ceiling"). When a ceiling effect occurs, interpretation of the data becomes difficult because the amount of variation in the variable being studied is reduced. This is especially important in assessing change over time.

Example Suppose a biology professor wants to find out whether increasing the amount of laboratory time in her courses will improve student scores on the examinations she gives. She therefore gives students in one of her classes 25% more lab time than she gives the students in the other class she teaches. She gives both classes a pretest to measure the initial level of student knowledge but finds that many of the students in the "extra lab time" class score at or near 100% on this pretest. She would not be able to tell, by making comparisons with posttest results, whether the extra lab time makes a difference or not, because the pretest scores of these students are so high (they hit the ceiling) that they can hardly go up any further (even if they learn a lot of biology during the term).

See also Skewed distribution; validity.

FIGURE 4.9 THE CEILING EFFECT

Reliability

Description   The consistency of a measure or instrument from one use to another. A reliable instrument is one that gives identical or very similar results in repeated measurements of the same thing.

Examples
- If you get on your bathroom scale and it reads 135 pounds, you get off and get on again and it reads 140 pounds, and you do this a third time and the scale reads 130 pounds, the scale (obviously) is not very reliable. On the other hand, if you weighed yourself a series of times and each time got the same result (say, 130 pounds), the scale would be reliable.

  Note that an instrument can be reliable yet not valid. For example, in repeated weighings, your scale might always read 130 pounds, even though your weight is actually 125 pounds. The results are consistent but not accurate (valid).

- A test development specialist constructs a new ninth-grade mathematics achievement test that has two equivalent forms, *A* and *B*. Both forms are intended to measure the same thing, and both are at the same level of difficulty. A large sample of ninth grade students answer *both* form *A* and form *B*. Results show that, with but a few exceptions, each student's score on form *A* is very close to his or her score on form *B*. The specialist concludes, therefore, that both forms of the test are reliable. (Note that this does not mean, however, that the two forms are *valid*—i.e., that they measure the knowledge and skills that they *should* measure.)

- Even such a clear-cut instrument as a carpenter's ruler can give unreliable measurements, since its use by different people can produce inconsistent results. While people are not likely to differ much when measuring to the quarter-inch, they may well differ when measuring to 1/64 of an inch.

See also   Validity.

FIGURE 4.10 RELIABILITY AND VALIDITY

Reliability Coefficient

Description   The **reliability coefficient** is a statistic indicating the reliability (i.e., the consistency) of a measurement under different circumstances, such as two measurements taken at different times; administered under changed environmental conditions; administered by different testers; or, in the case of many instruments used with people, involving tests on which the specific content differs.

Reliability coefficients are a particular application of the *correlation coefficient*. However, reliability coefficients range only from 0.00, indicating that the measure is completely unreliable, to 1.00, indicating perfect reliability. Negative values are meaningless. Reliability coefficients differ in different fields; for example, engineers commonly assume that their measurements are perfectly reliable ($R = 1.00$), although this may not be true. In measurements of people, a common rule of thumb is that a reliability coefficient above .90 is recommended for comparisons among individuals and a reliability coefficient of at least .70 for comparisons among groups. Clearly, higher is better.

Examples

- For most published ability tests, reliability coefficients that incorporate the circumstances listed above over a period of one year or less are usually near or above .90.

- Reliability coefficients for "personality" type instruments, even with time intervals of less than a few months, are often considerably below .90.

- Reliability coefficients for such common tests as the Snellen Eye Chart and blood pressure tests have often been reported as well below .90, which is why repeated testing is recommended.

See also   Correlation.

FIGURE 4.11   RELIABILITY OF A MEASUREMENT

Standard Error of Measurement

Description

The **standard error of measurement** is an index showing the extent to which a measurement would vary under changed circumstances. These variations are called *errors of measurement*. Since there are many ways in which measurement circumstances can change, such as the passage of time, environmental conditions, time of day, administrator, and, in the case of many instruments used with people, even the specific content, there are really many possible standard errors. The appropriate one to use depends on the way the measurement is interpreted. Under the assumption that errors of measurement are normally distributed, a range of scores within which a particular measurement will vary can be calculated.

Examples

- For many IQ tests, the standard error of measurement over a one-year period and with different specific content is about five points. Over a ten-year period, it is about eight points. This means that a score fluctuates considerably more the longer the time between measurements. Thus, a person scoring 110 can expect to have a score between 100 and 120 one year later; five years later, the score can be expected to be between 94 and 126. Note that we doubled the standard errors of measurement in computing the ranges within which the second score is expected to fall. This was done so we could be 95% sure that our reasoning was correct.

- The measurement of business sales on a daily basis will vary more than the average daily sales calculated on a monthly basis. In either case, an index of variation is useful.

See also

Confidence interval; mean; standard deviation.

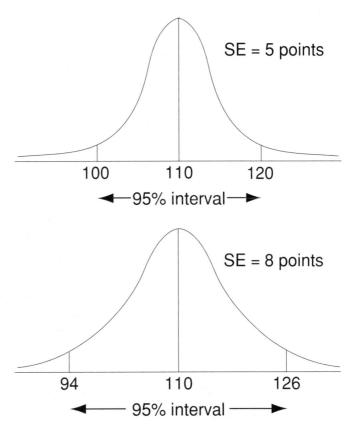

FIGURE 4.12 STANDARD ERROR OF MEASUREMENT

Validity

Description   **Validity** refers to the degree to which *evidence* supports any inferences a researcher makes based on the data he or she collects using an instrument. Validity is the most important idea to consider in developing or selecting an instrument. More than anything else, we want the data collected through the use of an instrument to be accurate, meaningful, and useful. Some methods of assessing validity make use of *validity coefficients*—a special use of the *correlation coefficient*.

Examples
- To find out what the members of a union think about a recent policy instituted by the union's governing board, we need both an instrument to record the data (their opinions) and some sort of assurance that the information we collect will enable us to draw correct conclusions about the opinions of the membership on this issue. The drawing of correct conclusions based on the data obtained is what validity is all about.

- Asking someone to tell us what he or she knows about how to drive a car would not usually be a valid way to find out whether the person actually *can* drive a car.

- Sometimes test developers modify an achievement test so it will be more homogeneous—in order to make it more reliable. In other words, it is changed so it will measure a narrower range of knowledge and skills. This procedure often does result in higher reliability or consistency. It may, however, actually *reduce* the *validity* of the test if the instructional objectives that the test is supposed to measure are actually *broader* than the scope of the test after it was revised to make it more homogeneous. In other words, it no longer measures all of what the students were taught. The bottom line: Reliability is important, but validity is more important than reliability.

- Instruments do not always measure what they seem to. Psychologists have debated for years the extent to which IQ scores measure "native intelligence," acquired skills, academic background, cultural differences and/or attitudes toward testing.

See also   Reliability.

TABLE 4.3 Valid versus Invalid Measurement

Measurement Objective	Likely to Be Valid, at Least to Some Degree	Likely to Be Invalid
What eighth graders know about the causes of the Civil War	25 multiple-choice questions, each dealing with one or more causes of the war	50 multiple-choice questions about the battles in the war
Ability to tune an automobile engine	Performance test that requires an individual to actually tune an engine	Paper-and-pencil test about how to tune an auto engine
To identify feelings of hostility	Projective test that asks people to describe their feelings when presented with abstract forms and shapes	Essay exam asking individual to write on the topic "Why I am hostile"

Norm

Description A **norm** is a reference for interpreting scores. Norms are determined by recording the scores of a large group of individuals (i.e., a large sample) who take a test of some sort. These scores then represent the "norm" (or standard) against which the scores of other individuals who take the test can be compared. The test is considered to be a "standardized," or "norm-referenced," test. The mean, or the median, of the scores of the large group is often used as the numerical value of the norm.

Example Both the Scholastic Aptitude Test (SAT) and the Graduate Record Examination (GRE) are examples of norm-referenced tests. A particular individual's score on either of these tests is an indication of how well he or she did in comparison to a large group of individuals who had taken the test previously; this previous group of test-takers was used to determine the norm or standard for the test. When someone says therefore that Joe scored "above the norm," this means that he did better than average (i.e., better than most of the students who took the test in the first place).

See also Mean; median; standard score.

FIGURE 4.13 WHAT'S THE NORM?

Nominal Scale/Level of Measurement

Description A **nominal scale** is a scale of measurement in which numbers stand for names but have no order or value. (Some statisticians do not even consider this to be measuring!) It is the simplest form of measurement that one can use. The use of a nominal scale involves nothing more than labeling and counting. It is, of course, possible and often useful to count the number of items in each category.

Examples
- Categorizing girls (as category 1) and boys (as category 2) in an elementary school classroom. Girls are not higher than boys; they do not come first; two girls do not add up to one boy; and so forth.
- Numbers may occasionally be useful identifiers, as in assigning numbers to the positions on a football team. Numbers ending in 8, such as 28, for example, are used to identify wide receivers.
- To save space, and to reduce the number of strokes in keyboarding at the computer, numbers may be used to identify the marital status of individuals: (1) married, (2) single, (3) widower, (4) widow, (5) separated, (6) divorce pending, and (7) divorced.

See also Interval scale; ordinal scale; ratio scale.

(a) Gender

(b) What's in a number?

FIGURE 4.14 NOMINAL SCALES

Ordinal Scale/Level of Measurement

Description An **ordinal scale** is a scale of measurement that ranks or orders data in some way (e.g., from high to low, from least to most). Ordinal scales are used to indicate the relative position, or rank order, of individuals in relation to each other.

Examples

- College basketball teams and professional tennis players are ranked every year. The rank of 1 is assigned to the team or player with the best record; the rank of 2 to the second best, the rank of 3 to the third best, and so forth. Notice that the difference in actual ability between the players or teams ranked 1 and 2 and that between those ranked 5 and 6 are most likely *not* the same. Therefore ordinal numbers should not be added, subtracted, multiplied, or divided, except in a few special cases such as *Spearman rank-order correlation*. While rankings do reflect more or less of something, they do not indicate *how much* more or less.

- Let us consider the hypothetical horse race in Figure 4.15 for another example of ordinal measurement. Eager Beaver came in first, Greased Lightning came in second, and Early Riser came in third. Dobbin, pulling a wagon, wasn't even in the race, but he got so excited when he saw the other horses running that his driver couldn't stop him from running. Regrettably (to both horse and driver), Dobbin and his wagon finished in a distant fourth place. As you can see, ranks of 1, 2, 3, and 4 can be assigned to the horses to indicate the order in which they finished the race. However, these ranks say nothing about the actual distance that existed between the horses as they crossed the finish line. Greased Lightning, for example, was very close to Eager Beaver at the finish, but the distance between Greased Lightning and Early Riser was considerably greater.

See also Interval scale; nominal scale; ratio scale.

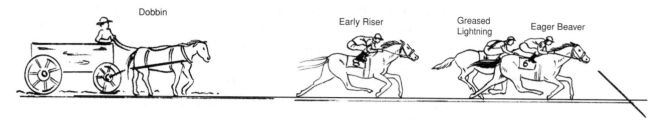

FIGURE 4.15   AN ORDINAL SCALE: THE WINNER OF A HORSE RACE

Interval Scale/Level of Measurement

Description   An **interval scale** is a scale of measurement that describes variables in such a way that the distance between any two adjacent units (or intervals) of measurement is equal to the distance between any other two adjacent units but in which there is no meaningful zero point. Scores on an interval scale can be added and subtracted, but they cannot be multiplied or divided. It is quite desirable to have an interval scale when making measurements, and many statistical operations require the assumption that an interval scale is being used.

Examples

- The units for scores on most commercially available mathematics achievement tests are usually considered (but not known) to be equal in size throughout the low, middle, and high parts of the scale. Thus, the difference between a score of 45 and one of 55 is considered to be the same difference in ability as the difference between a score of 80 and one of 90. If this is true, differences between scores on such a test can be interpreted as meaningful differences in ability. However, a score of zero on such a test does not mean that the student has absolutely zero knowledge of mathematics. It may be that he or she could correctly answer many mathematics questions at a more elementary level than those on the test on which he or she received a zero. Therefore, this problem of interval scale measurement makes it illogical to say that a student who receives a score of 80 knows twice as much as a student who receives a score of 40.

- Both the Fahrenheit and Celsius temperature scales are examples of interval scales. Although the size of unit is different on the two scales, the units in each are of *equal size* all along the scale. Consider the Fahrenheit scale. A difference in amount of heat between 25° and 30° on this scale is equal to the difference between 85° and 90°. This means that differences in Fahrenheit readings can be compared. Similar observations can be made of the Celsius scale. Neither scale has a true zero (i.e., a complete absence of temperature).

See also   Nominal scale; ordinal scale; ratio scale.

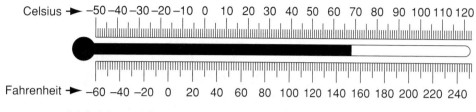

(a) Celsius and Fahrenheit Temperature Scales

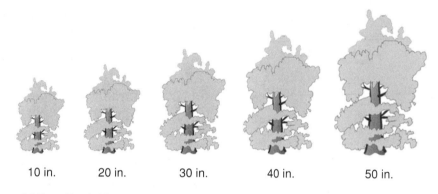

10 in.   20 in.   30 in.   40 in.   50 in.

(b) Tree Trunk Measurements

FIGURE 4.16   INTERVAL SCALES

Ratio Scale/Level of Measurement

Description A **ratio scale** has all of the characteristics of an interval scale and, in addition, a true zero point. Any two adjoining values are the same distance apart, all along the scale. Measurements obtained from a ratio scale can be added, subtracted, multiplied, and divided. It is the most useful of the four levels of measurement, because it permits statements about multiples and ratios. In fact, the scale gets its name from the fact that *ratio* statements can be made about variables that are measured on such a scale.

Examples
- A ruler used for measuring length. Note that the size of the units all along the ruler are equal and that the zero point represents zero (i.e., *no*) length.
- A bathroom scale. The zero on this scale means *no* weight.
- A speedometer. The zero on this scale means the car is *stopped* (i.e., zero speed).
- A tire gauge. The zero on this scale indicates *no* pressure.
- The absolute temperature scale. This scale has both equal units all along the scale and a true zero point. Zero on this scale is the temperature at which there is absolutely no heat. It corresponds to –459.67 degrees Fahrenheit.

See also Interval scale; nominal scale; ordinal scale.

FIGURE 4.17 A RATIO SCALE

EXPERIMENTATION

PART III

Set 5

Does taking an aspirin every day decrease a person's chance of having a heart attack? Does attaching a nicotine patch to the skin help someone to quit smoking? One way to get answers to these questions is to ask some people to take an aspirin, or wear a nicotine patch, and find out what happens. In each case, we'd have an *experiment*. We also could simply survey a sample of people who take aspirin regularly or who have tried a nicotine patch and ask about their effect. This would not be an experiment. An experiment, if set up correctly, will tell us more about the effect of a treatment of some sort (e.g., taking aspirin regularly or wearing a nicotine patch) than will just surveying a sample. Designing a good experiment is no easy matter. In this section, we describe and illustrate several of the more important concepts involved in the experimental process.

Experiments

Concepts in This Set

Listed Sequentially

experiment
dependent/independent variables
treatment
control group
placebo
extraneous variable
confounding
double-blind procedure
matched pairs design
block design
observational study
Hawthorne effect

Listed Alphabetically

block design
confounding
control group
dependent/independent variables
double-blind procedure
experiment
extraneous variable
Hawthorne effect
matched pairs design
observational study
placebo
treatment

Experiment

Description   An **experiment** is a type of study in which a researcher deliberately manipulates an independent (sometimes called *treatment* or *experimental*) variable. The purpose of the manipulation is to observe what changes (if any) occur in one or more dependent variables (sometimes called *outcome* or *criterion* variables). *Random assignment* of subjects to experimental and control groups is viewed as essential if a true experiment is to take place. An experiment is the most powerful method available to scientists for studying cause-and-effect relationships.

Example   The Physician's Health Study was a medical experiment designed to investigate the question "Does the regular taking of aspirin protect individuals against the occurrence of a heart attack?" Half of a group of 22,000 male physicians were randomly selected to take an aspirin every other day. The other 11,000 of these physicians took a *placebo,* a fake pill that looked and tasted like aspirin but actually had no active ingredient. Both groups of physicians took a pill every other day, and all of them got the same number of checkups and were given the same instructions. Presumably the only difference was the content of the pills. After several years, 239 of the physicians in the placebo group, but only 139 of those in the aspirin group had experienced a heart attack.[1] The independent variable is whether the subject took aspirin or a placebo; the dependent variable is whether or not the subject had a heart attack. Note that it is the active application of a treatment, not merely the presence of an independent and a dependent variable, that makes a study an experiment.

See also   Confounding; dependent/independent variable; extraneous variable; matched pairs design; observational study; substantive significance; statistical significance.

---

[1]Steering Committee of the Physician's Health Study Research Group. "Final Report on the Aspirin Component of the Ongoing Physician's Health Study." (1989). *New England Journal of Medicine,* vol. 321, pp. 129–135.

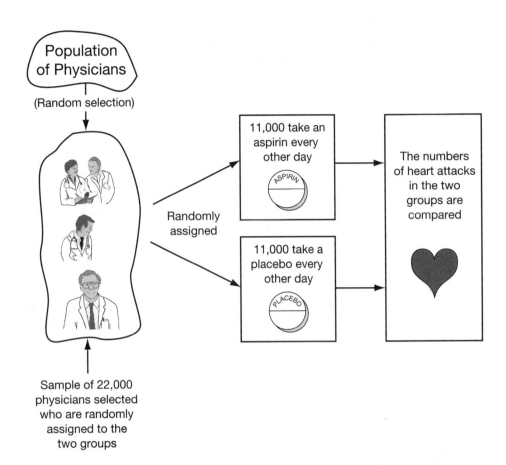

Population
of Physicians

(Random selection)

11,000 take an aspirin every other day

ASPIRIN

11,000 take a placebo every other day

PLACEBO

The numbers of heart attacks in the two groups are compared

Randomly assigned

Sample of 22,000 physicians selected who are randomly assigned to the two groups

Dependent/Independent Variables

Description   A **dependent variable** (sometimes called an *outcome* or *response* variable), is one that is (or is thought to be) influenced by one or more other variables. Variables that affect dependent variables are called **independent variables.** An easy way to remember the distinction between the two is to think of dependent variables as those that "depend on" what happens with other (independent) variables.

   The use of these terms—dependent variable and independent variable—is not limited to experiments. Sometimes the independent variable, for example, is a variable that is only "thought" to influence a dependent variable. Usage is most clear, however, with respect to experimental studies.

Examples
- In driving a car the amount of gas consumed is dependent upon the number of miles driven. The dependent variable is *number of gallons of gas consumed,* and the independent variable is *number of miles driven.*
- A favorite area of study for psychologists is the relationship between frustration and aggression. What they are interested in is whether being frustrated leads to aggressive behavior. In such instances, the dependent variable is *extent of aggressive behavior,* and the independent variable is *degree of frustration.*
- Several types and dosages of medication are available for reducing high blood pressure. The dependent variable would be *blood pressure level;* the independent variables would be *type and dosage* of medication.
- The distance a runner covers depends on the speed at which she jogs and the length of time she runs. The dependent variable here is *distance;* the independent variables are *speed* and *time.*

See also   Double-blind procedure; experiment; observational study; treatment; variable.

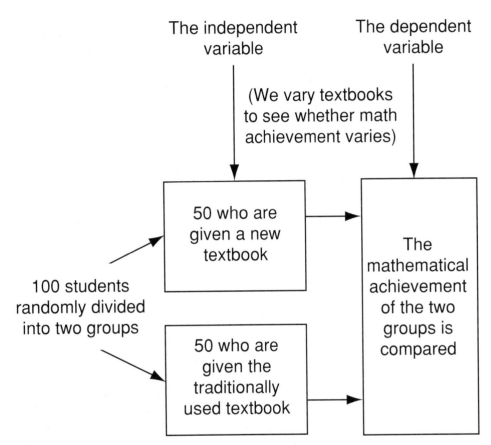

FIGURE 5.2 MATHEMATICAL ACHIEVEMENT SHOWN AS A DEPENDENT VARIABLE

Treatment

Description In an experiment, a **treatment** is what is given to the subjects in the experimental group but not to those in the control group. A treatment creates an independent variable. If an experiment has several independent variables, a treatment is a combination of specific values of these variables. Treatments at times consist of *levels,* as when subjects are given different amounts of medication to compare their effects on reducing swelling or other ailments.

Examples
- Psychologists who are interested in the effects of the violence in television cartoons on young children might select a random sample of six-year-olds at a daycare center and observe them interacting in their play groups. They might then divide the children into two groups and show a videotape of a violent cartoon program to half (the experimental group) and a non-violent program to the other half (the control group). The children could then again be observed interacting in their play groups. Note that the treatment in this experiment is the showing of the videotape of the violent cartoon program.

- The Physician's Health Study to which we referred (see Figure 5.1 on page 147) looked at the effects of not only aspirin, but also beta carotene. (Beta carotene is converted by the body into Vitamin A, which researchers believe may help to prevent various types of cancer.) Thus, both aspirin and beta carotene were treatments in the study. Figure 5.3 illustrates how they were combined.

See also Control group; dependent/independent variable; experiment.

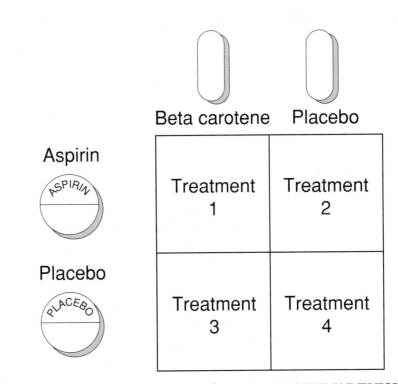

FIGURE 5.3 THE PHYSICIAN'S HEALTH STUDY REVISITED

Control Group

Description

In experimental research, a **control group** is a group that receives either no treatment or a neutral "placebo" treatment. The purpose of a control group is to provide a basis for comparison with the experimental group. In many experimental studies, in fact, there is no control group, but rather one or more *comparison groups* that receive a *different* treatment rather than no treatment at all.

Examples

- Psychologists studying the effects of films on attitudes toward racial discrimination might give a group of individuals a pretest (a questionnaire) to measure their attitudes, divide the group in two, and then show an antidiscrimination film to one half. A neutral film would be shown to the other half (the control group). A second questionnaire could then be given to the two groups to determine whether the films had any effect on their responses.

- A high school history teacher wonders if the playing of classical music during examinations would lessen the anxiety that many students experience during the taking of tests. She decides to play some music by Tchaikowsky in one of her classes (but not in another), while the members of the class are taking a unit test, measuring in both instances the student's anxiety level both before and after taking the test. The "no-music" class is the control group.

- Environmental scientists who study grazing impacts on plant life might compare rangeland grazed: (a) only by elk; (b) only by cattle; and (c) by both elk and cattle. Each treatment would be arranged and implemented as part of the study. The experiemental group would (probably) be the "cattle-only" condition, since the other treatments occur naturally. Conditions (a) and (c), therefore, are the comparison groups.

See also Dependent/independent variable; experiment; treatment.

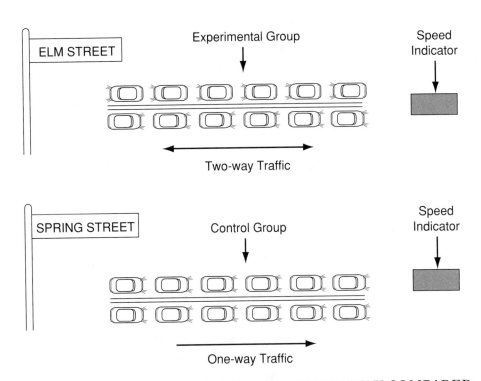

FIGURE 5.4   HOW FAST DO CARS GO ON ONE-WAY COMPARED TO TWO-WAY STREETS?

Placebo

Description   A **placebo** is a dummy treatment, that is, a treatment given in an experiment to a control group. It is meant to have no effect but is used to permit comparison with the treatment (given to the experimental group) that is actually being investigated.

The main reason for using a placebo is that sometimes people and animals (and maybe even plants) show change or improvement as a result of increased attention or recognition just because they are part of a study. In medicine, belief in a treatment (any treatment) may result in improvment.

Examples
- In an experiment designed to test the effects of a new drug that is intended to promote weight loss, the experimental group would be given the new drug, while the control group could be given a sugar pill. The sugar pill would be the placebo.
- In the Physician's Health Study to which we referred earlier (see Figure 5.1), half of a group of 22,000 male physicians took an aspirin every other day, while the other half took a fake pill that looked and tasted like aspirin, but actually had no active ingredient. This fake pill was a placebo.
- In an experiment to assess the effectiveness of a new medication on the rapidity with which the AIDS virus spreads, one randomly selected group of subjects is given a fake pill—a placebo—that contains no medication, but is otherwise identical to the pill containing the medication.

See also   Experiment; treatment.

FIGURE 5.5   A PLACEBO

Extraneous Variable

Description   **Extraneous variables** (sometimes referred to as *uncontrolled variables, lurking variables,* or *nuisance variables*), are troublesome influences (independent variables) that affect research results in ways that can place conclusions in doubt. If such variables are not controlled or accounted for, alternative explanations can be advanced as to why the results turned out as they did. Extraneous variables can affect one or more dependent variables in ways that obscure or distort measurement and/or interpretation of the results obtained in a study. Researchers try to control for extraneous variables primarily through randomization, holding them constant, or some statistical technique such as *analysis of covariance.*

Example   Standardized achievement test results are often analyzed to make comparisons among the schools in a district and among school districts. Conclusions from such studies sometimes suggest that schools and districts with low average scores have ineffective teachers or are poorly managed. But a number of extraneous variables can influence how much children learn in school. These include their parents' attitude toward education, their social class, the number of books in the home, their family's income level, and the presence of problems in the home such as alcoholism or mental illness.

See also   Dependent/independent variable; Simpson's paradox; variable.

The principal of a junior high school compares the final examination scores of two biology teachers, not realizing that they are not comparable in many respects because of *extraneous variables*. The classes differ in

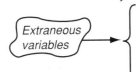

- gender of students
- gender of teacher
- age of teacher
- time of day class meets
- days of week class meets
- ethnicity of teacher

Ms. Brown's (age 31) biology class meets from 9:00 to 9:50 A.M. Tuesdays and Thursdays. The class contains 16 students, all girls.

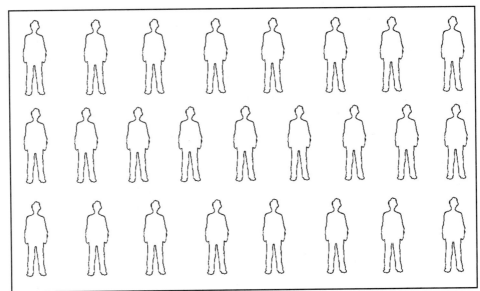

Mr. Thompson's (age 54) biology class meets from 2:00 to 3:00 P.M. Mondays and Wednesdays. The class contains 25 students, all boys.

FIGURE 5.6   EXTRANEOUS VARIABLES

Confounding

Description The effects of two independent variables on a dependent variable are said to be **confounded** when their effects cannot be distinguished from one another.

Examples

- Suppose one chemistry professor uses textbook A in his classes and another professor uses textbook B in her classes; then students are given an end-of-semester examination to see how much chemistry they have learned. The independent variables (the textbooks and the professors' teaching ability) would be *confounded*. There would be no way to tell whether any differences in achievement between the two classes on the end-of-semester examination (the dependent variable) were caused by either or both of the independent variables.

- If surgeons use a general anesthetic for difficult operations (e.g., multiple bypass heart surgery) with very ill patients and a spinal anesthetic for relatively simpler operations (e.g., removal of a hydrocele in the scrotum), there will be more complications (even death) as a result of using the general anesthetic. The type of anesthesia is *confounded* with the type of surgery, making it difficult to determine the direct effect of the anesthetic on the results of the surgery.

- Alice Adams finds that the grass in her front yard is very lush and green this year after she waters her lawn with a new brand of fertilizer, which must be mixed with water beforehand. Accordingly, she urges all of her friends to use this fertilizer. Is her praise warranted? Maybe. But maybe not. Since the fertilizer must be applied with water, the effects of extra watering and fertilizing are confounded.

See also Dependent/independent variable; extraneous variable; Simpson's paradox; variable.

FIGURE 5.7 CONFOUNDING

Double-Blind Procedure

Description   The **double-blind procedure** is a way to reduce bias in an experiment by making sure that *both* the administrators and the recipients of the treatment do not know (are "blind" to) which subjects are in the experimental group and which are in the control group—that is, who is and who is not receiving the treatment.

Example   Suppose a researcher wishes to study the effectiveness of various commercial remedies for minor aches and pains. She selects a random sample of 100 subjects from a population of soldiers at a military base and randomly assigns them to four groups. Group 1 receives Tylenol; group 2 receives Advil; group 3 receives aspirin; and group 4 receives a placebo. The pills are all identical in shape and size so that the researcher's assistant, who is handing them out, will not know which group is getting which pill and so that the subjects will not know what pill they are getting. When a subject complains of pain (e.g., headache), he or she will be given the appropriate pill depending on the group and then asked how much (if any) relief he or she got from the pill. The responses will then be the *data* the researchers will use to judge the effectiveness of the different remedies. Furthermore, the researcher will not be told which group received which pill until after the data are analyzed and a conclusion is reached as to which pill was the most effective.

See also   Control group; dependent/independent variable; experiment; extraneous variable; matched pairs design; observational study; placebo.

FIGURE 5.8 A DOUBLE-BLIND EXPERIMENT

Matched Pairs Design

Description   In a **matched pairs design** (also known as *matched subjects, related samples,* and *correlated samples* designs), pairs of individual subjects are matched on characteristics that might affect their reaction to a treatment. After the pairs are determined, ideally one member of each pair is randomly assigned to the experimental group (the group that is getting the treatment). Without random assignment, matching is not as effective. The variable or variables used in matching are those that the researcher wishes to control. In some studies, more than two groups are involved; some may have two (or even more) experimental groups and one control group. The matching procedures, however, are the same as for those described above for pair matching in two-group studies.

Example   Imagine an experiment to determine the effectiveness of a face cream for removing wrinkles. One group of women (the experimental group) is asked to use the cream daily, and the other (the control group) is given another cream to use daily that is known to have no effect on wrinkles. The groups are formed by first identifying matching pairs of women of the same age, state of general health, color of skin, extent of wrinkling, and approximate levels of exposure to the sun. After the pairs are identified, pair members are randomly assigned (pair by pair) to the experimental and control groups. Imagine the dismay of the face cream company (the sponsors of the experiment) if the experimental face cream does not remove any wrinkles!

See also   Control group; dependent/independent variable; extraneous variable; treatment.

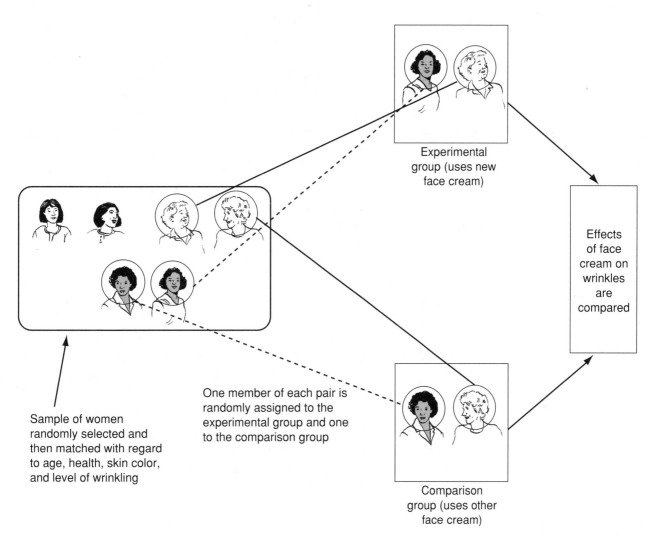

Experimental
group (uses new
face cream)

Effects
of face
cream on
wrinkles
are
compared

One member of each pair is
randomly assigned to the
experimental group and one
to the comparison group

Sample of women
randomly selected and
then matched with regard
to age, health, skin color,
and level of wrinkling

Comparison
group (uses other
face cream)

FIGURE 5.9 A MATCHED PAIRS DESIGN

Block Design

Description A **block** is a group of subjects (or other experimental units) that are similar in some way that can affect the outcome of an experiment. In a *randomized complete block design,* the subjects are first *nonrandomly* divided into blocks according to an extraneous variable that the experimenter seeks to control. Then, *within each* block, the subjects are randomly assigned to different treatments. Each block in a randomized complete block design contains the same number of subjects and the same number of treatments. Block designs are a way of holding constant an extraneous variable that otherwise might cause large variations in the experimental results. One frequently used type of block design is the *matched pairs design.*

Example ▪ A physician designs a study to find out whether a vitamin supplement taken daily will lower the blood pressure of 100 people 65 years of age and older who have high blood pressure. Preliminary studies indicate that it may indeed be effective and that the effect may be greater for women than for men. The physician sets up two blocks, each consisting of 50 individuals, grouping the subjects by gender. He then randomly assigns half of the men and half of the women to take the vitamin supplement and the other half to take a placebo. He records the changes that occur in blood pressure after a suitable period of time (say, 6 to 8 weeks or so).

See also Control group; dependent/independent variable; extraneous variable; experiment; matched pairs design; treatment.

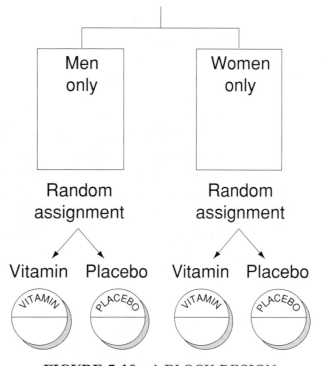

FIGURE 5.10   A BLOCK DESIGN

Observational Study

Description   In an **observational study,** in contrast to an *experiment*, researchers observe individuals and record what they see occurring but do not attempt to impose a treatment, manipulate conditions, or influence responses in any way. The essential purpose of an observational study is to describe, accurately and carefully, the activities of a group or situation.

Examples
- The most common treatment for breast cancer that is detected early was once a mastectomy (removal of the breast). It is now more common to remove the tumor and the nearby lymph nodes and then to administer radiation to the surrounding area. To study the comparative effectiveness of these two treatments, a medical research team examines the health records at a large hospital of 200 women, half having had a mastectomy and the other half having had the newer approach.

- A researcher is interested in the ways preschoolers interact on the playground. She unobtrusively observes a group of 3–4 year-olds enrolled in a day care center playing in a sandbox. This, too, is an observational study. The children are not imposed on or manipulated in any way.

- Foresters studying the effects of fire in preventing erosion are reluctant to create large-scale fires. Instead, they compare areas that have burned due to accidents or lightning with similar areas that have not burned. They conduct a detailed observation of soil, water, and plant conditions in both areas.

See also   Experiment; independent variable; treatment.

(a) An observational study of children in a schoolyard

(b) Observing animals in their natural habitat

(c) An observational study of reactions of children just before they get a tetanus shot

FIGURE 5.11 SOME OBSERVATIONAL STUDIES

Hawthorne Effect

Description The **Hawthorne effect** is a tendency for subjects in an experiment or other type of study to change their behavior just because they are being studied. It differs from other extraneous variables in that the effects are thought to be due simply to being part of a study, rather than to such things as beliefs about a particular treatment or the characteristics of the researchers.

Examples
- The first observation on record of this effect was in the Hawthorne plant of the Western Electric Company some years ago. It was accidentally discovered that worker productivity improved not just when improvements were made in the physical working conditions (such as better lighting and an increase in the number of coffee breaks), but also when the working conditions were unintentionally made *worse* (e.g., the number of coffee breaks was reduced and the lighting was dimmed). The usual explanation for this is that the workers felt they were getting special attention and recognition.
- If people realize they are being watched by their teachers, employers, or coaches, they often may perform better (or sometimes worse) than they would when they are not being observed. This change in behavior often is due to the Hawthorne effect.

See also Confounding; experiment; extraneous variable; treatment.

FIGURE 5.12 THE HAWTHORNE EFFECT

LOOKING FOR RELATIONSHIPS IN DATA

PART IV

Set 6

Much statistical analysis is concerned with relationships among two or more variables that are quantitative, that is, variables that exist in some degree or amount. The basic question is as follows: Is an increase or decrease on one variable accompanied by an increase or decrease on the other—or others? Studying this question requires understanding a number of concepts that are presented in this section.

Relationships between Quantitative Variables: Correlation

Concepts in This Set

Listed Sequentially

quantitative variable
continuous variable
positive correlation
negative correlation
x-y axes
scatterplot
outlier
correlation coefficient
biserial/point biserial correlation
Spearman rank-order correlation coefficient
restricted range effect
correlation ratio
multiple correlation
coefficient of determination
factor analysis
path analysis
partial correlation
correlation versus causation

Listed Alphabetically

biserial/point biserial correlation
coefficient of determination
continuous variable
correlation coefficient
correlation ratio
correlation versus causation
factor analysis
multiple correlation
negative correlation
outlier
partial correlation
path analysis
positive correlation
quantitative variable
restricted range effect
scatterplot
Spearman rank-order correlation coefficient
x-y axes

Quantitative Variable

Description A **quantitative variable** is a variable that exists in different degrees or quantities with a clear progression from "more" to "less," in contrast to categorical variables, which do not have this property. With categorical variables, the only things that can be done with individual pieces of data are to place them in categories and count them. They cannot be placed in order from "more" to "less," but quantitative variables can.

Examples Some quantitative variables are age, height, weight, mechanical aptitude, anxiety level, attitude toward religion, temperature, air pressure, distance, knowledge of history, aggressive behavior, blood pressure, white cell count, nutrient values, calorie level, population, income, sales, net profit, trees per acre, voting rate, vote count, product price, housing density, interest rate, and tax rate.

See also Categorical variable; discrete variable; variable.

(a) An Anxiety Scale

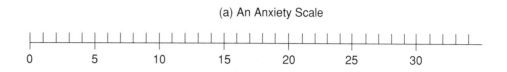

(b) Air Pressure Shown in Pounds per Square Inch

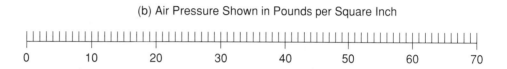

(c) Price of Houses in Thousands of Dollars

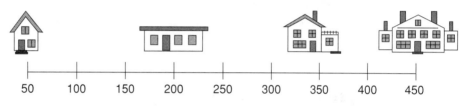

FIGURE 6.1   QUANTITATIVE VARIABLES

Continuous Variable

Description A **continuous variable** is a quantitative variable that can have an *unlimited* number of values between any two successive whole numbers, such as 34 and 35. Values such as 34.1, 34.999, and 34.2865409167 are possible, depending on the quality and accuracy of your measuring instrument and the precision of your computations. Regardless of how close together two numbers on a continuous variable are, it is possible to identify a number that falls between them. Numerical values of a continuous variable can be added, subtracted, multiplied, and divided.

Examples Measures of length, weight, time, atmospheric pressure, speed, and temperature are examples of continuous variables. The measurements can be expressed with as many decimal places as desired.

See also Categorical variable; quantitative variable; variable.

A continuous variable is measured by each
of the following kinds of instruments:

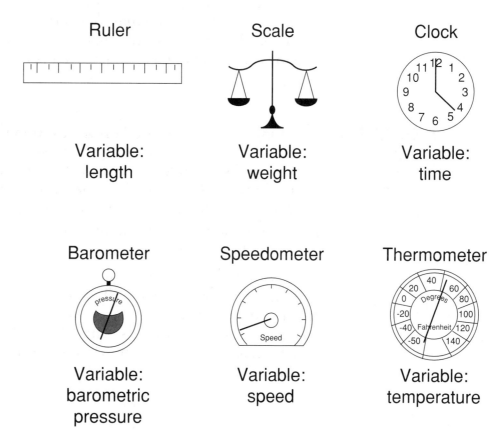

Ruler

Variable:
length

Scale

Variable:
weight

Clock

Variable:
time

Barometer

Variable:
barometric
pressure

Speedometer

Variable:
speed

Thermometer

Variable:
temperature

FIGURE 6.2   THE MEASUREMENT OF CONTINUOUS VARIABLES

Positive Correlation

Description A **positive correlation** is a relationship between two variables such that, whenever the value of one goes up (i.e., increases), so does the other. Similarly, whenever the value of one variable goes down (i.e., decreases), so does the other. This is sometimes called a *direct correlation*. Note that to determine whether (or what kind of) a correlation exists, we must have a score for *each* characteristic on *each* individual or object that is being studied.

Examples
- Study time and scores on an examination: The amount of study time that students put in before an examination and their subsequent scores on that examination likely are positively related; that is, in general, the more hours a student studies, the higher his or her exam score will be.
- Height and weight: Generally, the taller a person is, the more he or she weighs.

Correlations are rarely, if ever, perfect. Exceptions exist in practically all relationships between variables. Thus, although taller people, in general, tend to weigh more than shorter people, there are some individuals who are tall but who do not weigh much because they are thin, while some are short but weigh a lot because they are fat.

See also Correlation coefficient; multiple correlation; negative correlation; variable.

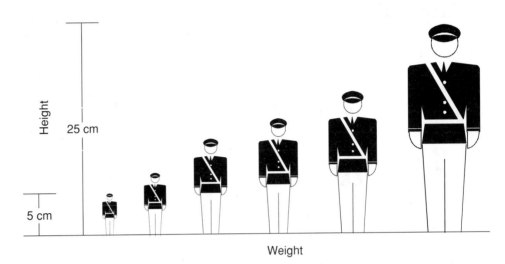

FIGURE 6.3 A POSITIVE CORRELATION BETWEEN HEIGHT AND WEIGHT

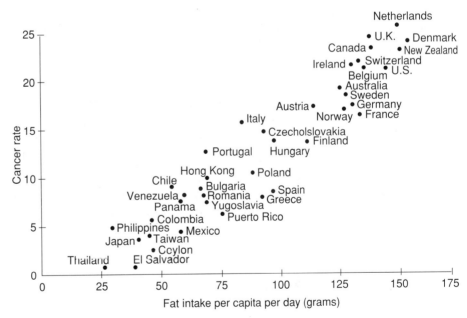

FIGURE 6.4 CANCER RATES PLOTTED AGAINST FAT IN THE DIET: A POSITIVE CORRELATION

Source: E.K. Carroll, "Experimental evidence of dietary factors and hormone-dependent cancers." *Cancer Research* vol. 35 (1975) p. 3379. Copyright by *Cancer Research*.

Negative Correlation

Description   A **negative correlation** is a relationship between two variables such that whenever one increases, the other decreases. This is sometimes called an inverse correlation. Note that to determine whether (or what kind) of correlation exists, we must have a score for *each* characteristic on *each* individual or object that is being studied.

Examples
- Volume and pressure: As the volume of a closed cylinder containing a gas *decreases*, the pressure inside the cylinder *increases* (i.e., a decrease in volume goes with an increase in pressure, and vice versa).

- Mileage driven and tire tread: The *fewer* number of miles a tire has been driven, the *thicker* is the tread on the tire (i.e., low mileage goes with high thickness of tread, and vice versa).

- The 11 candles shown in Figure 6.5 were all of the same height and diameter before they were lit. Each was lit at a different time (except the first one on the left, which was not lit at all). All of the remaining 10 were blown out at the same time. The number of minutes that each candle was allowed to burn and a measure of the height (in centimeters) of the candle are listed below each.

    As you can see, the greater the time in minutes that a candle burned, the smaller is its height in centimeters, even though some burned a little faster or slower than others. This inverse relationship illustrates a negative correlation between burning time and height of the candles. When we calculated the correlation coefficient, we found it to be −0.989, indicating a very strong negative correlation (but not a perfect one because, as one might expect, the candles did not all get shorter at exactly the same rate).

See also   Positive correlation.

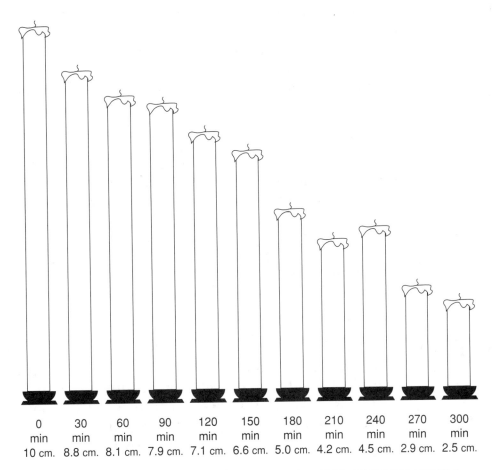

FIGURE 6.5   A VERY STRONG NEGATIVE CORRELATION

FIGURE 6.6   A PERFECT NEGATIVE CORRELATION

x-y Axes

Description The ***x-y* axes** are used in graphs to represent two sets of numbers at the same time. The x-axis is drawn horizontally; the y-axis is perpendicular to the x-axis. Both axes are scales on which distances correspond to the sizes of numbers that are represented on the graph. The point where the two axes intersect is called the *origin,* which corresponds to the value of zero on both axes. The positive direction is to the right on the x-axis and upward on the y-axis. Each pair of values is represented by *one* dot on the graph. The distances of the dot from the two axes represent the sizes of the two numerical values. The distance (measured along the x-axis) from the vertical axis is called the *abscissa*. The distance (measured along the y-axis) from the horizontal axis is called the *ordinate*. Many x-y graphs represent positive numbers only. In such cases, the origin and the y-axis are on the extreme left side of the graph, and there are no dots below the x-axis.

Examples
- A common use of x-y axes is in geographical location, both international (latitude and longitude) and locally. All land areas in the United States can be divided into sections identified by "township" on the x-axis and "range" on the y-axis. By using these (or more precise numbers), any particular spot in a country can be identified—e.g., Township 16 North, Range 3 East.
- Bar graphs, histograms, frequency polygons, and scatterplots all have horizontal and vertical axes. They are not, however, always labeled x and y.

See also Bar graph; histogram; frequency polygon; scatterplot.

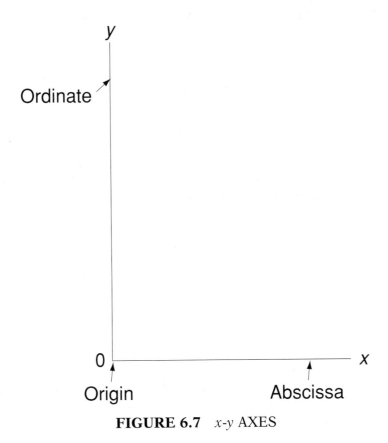

FIGURE 6.7 *x-y* AXES

Scatterplot

Description **Scatterplots** (also called *scattergrams* or *scatter diagrams*) show the pattern of points that result when two quantitative variables are plotted against each other on a graph. Each point or dot represents the scores of one individual on the two variables; it is where the lines representing the values of the two variables intersect.

    The pattern of the points indicates not only the strength, but also the direction, of the relationship between the two variables. The more the points tend to cluster together around a straight line, the stronger is the relationship between the variables (the higher the correlation). If the line around which the dots cluster runs from lower left to upper right, the relationship shown in the scatterplot is positive; if it runs from upper left to lower right, the relationship is negative. If the dots are scattered randomly throughout the plot, then the relationship between the variables is likely to be zero, or close to it. A scatterplot, therefore, is a pictorial representation of a *correlation*.

Example A scatterplot showing the relationship between grade point average and ratings of people's artistic ability ($r = .37$) is shown in Figure 6.8.

See also Correlation; correlation coefficient; negative correlation; positive correlation.

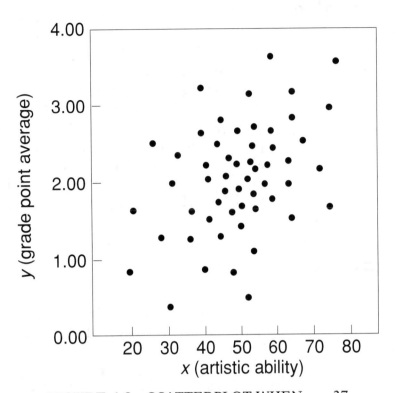

FIGURE 6.8   SCATTERPLOT WHEN $r = .37$

Outlier

Description

Outliers are scores or measurements that are different by such large amounts from those of other individuals in a group that they must be given careful consideration as special cases. They indicate an unusual exception to a general pattern. They may indicate an exceptionally high (e.g., genius) level—or a pathologically low measure—of some kind of ability.

Frequency distribution tables, histograms, and frequency polygons should be examined routinely for such outliers. They also sometimes occur in scatterplots. Any tally marks for frequencies that are located an unusually long distance from the others in the closer grouping of frequencies should be noted.

Example

Table 6.1 shows the scores of a group of individuals taking a drivers' test.

Note that all but one of the scores are rather closely bunched together between 40 and 99. However, one person scored *much* lower than the others, with a score somewhere between 10 and 19. That score is an outlier. Perhaps someone should try to find the reason for the low score. Was the person feeling ill that day? Did he or she not understand the directions? Was an error made in scoring the test? If no such factors were involved, the score may actually be an accurate measure of the person's knowledge.

Figure 6.9 shows the relationship between gross sales and net profit for a group of businesses. Notice the lonely business near the upper left-hand corner of the figure. It indicates a business that had high sales but low profit. The reasons why should be of interest to the sales manager!

See also

Correlation; frequency distribution; scatterplot.

TABLE 6.1 Scores on a Drivers' Test

Scores	Frequency
90–99	2
80–89	3
70–79	5
60–69	6
50–59	7
40–49	4
30–39	0
20–29	0
10–19	1 ◄——— Outlier
Total	28

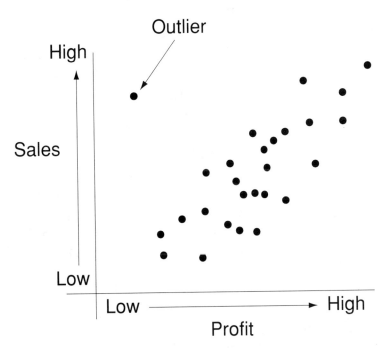

FIGURE 6.9 RELATIONSHIP BETWEEN SALES AND PROFIT IN A HYPOTHETICAL GROUP OF COMPANIES

Correlation Coefficient

Description A **correlation coefficient** is a number that is used to show the degree to which two quantitative variables are related. Correlation coefficients range from –1.00 to +1.00, are usually reported to two decimal places, and are symbolized by the lowercase letter r. If there is a perfect negative correlation between A and B, whenever A is high, B is low, and vice versa. If there is a perfect positive correlation between A and B, whenever one is high or low, so is the other. A correlation of 0.00 means that there is no relationship between the variables. There are numerous ways to calculate correlation coefficients, depending on the nature of the variables being studied; the most common is Pearson's r. Interpretation of correlation coefficients is best communicated by means of scatterplots as shown in Figure 6.10. The use of the correlation coefficients shown in Figure 6.10 assumes that the relationship is best described by a straight line.

Examples
- We would expect an r of .80 between aggressive driving and community size—a high positive correlation (since we think that increased population density leads to more aggressive driving).

- We would expect an r of .60 between free-throw-shooting percentages and field goal percentages among professional basketball players—a moderately high positive correlation.

- We would expect an r of .30 between years of schooling and income—a low positive correlation.

- We would expect an r of .15 between housing prices and number of building regulations—a very low positive correlation.

- We would expect an r of –.50 between amount of rainfall and price of grain—a moderately negative correlation (since we would expect increased production to drive prices down).

- We would expect an r of –.70 between amount of available land and price of lots—a fairly high negative correlation.

See also Correlation versus causation; negative correlation; positive correlation.

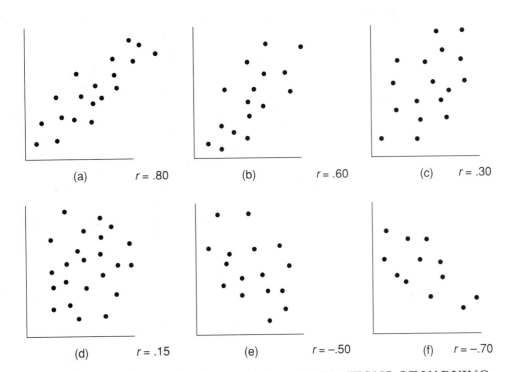

FIGURE 6.10 SCATTERPLOTS OF CORRELATIONS OF VARYING
STRENGTH

Biserial/Point Biserial Correlation

Description   **Biserial correlation** and **point biserial correlation** are procedures for determining the relationships between a continuous variable and a dichotomous variable. In the biserial correlation, the dichotomous variable is assumed to be actually a continuous variable that has been collapsed to only two levels and that both variables are normally distributed (conform to the bell-shaped normal curve). The point biserial correlation procedure does not make these assumptions. The biserial correlation gives an estimate of what the correlation would have been if the collapsed dichotomous variable had been left as a continuous variable, although this estimate is usually high. The biserial correlation coefficient is always larger than the point biserial correlation coefficient.

Examples

- One or the other of these methods of biserial correlation can be used to determine correlations such as those between (a) students' right or wrong answers on a test (assigning a 1 for right and a 0 for wrong) and their total scores on the test; (b) gender (assigning a 1 for male and a 0 for female) and income; (c) political party affiliation (assigning a 1 for Republican and a 0 for Democrat) and age of the individual; and (d) size of periodontal pocket and presence or absence of a toothache (assigning a 1 for presence and a 0 for absence).

- It is often assumed that the scoring of educational test questions as either right or wrong is an unavoidable simplification of a continuous variable, since there are undoubtedly degrees of understanding among individuals, ranging from "no idea whatsoever" to "almost correct," as well as degrees of "correctness." The biserial correlation is commonly calculated in such instances.

  On the other hand, if 0 and 1 are used to represent the absence or presence of a condition such as owning or not owning a car, the point biserial is probably the correct statistic to use in calculating the correlation between car ownership and gender.

- Notice that more of the students in Table 6.2 who received high total scores on a civics test answered item 12 correctly than did those who received low total scores. This suggests that the correlation coefficient will be positive, and it is. The computed value for the biserial coefficient is 0.48, and that for the point biserial coefficient is 0.38.

TABLE 6.2 Scores of 14 Students on a Civics Test

Student's Name	Total Test Score	Score on Item 12
Jamal	98	1
George	86	1
Rachel	80	1
Seth	74	0
Maria	69	0
Jane	61	1
Henry	61	0
Celeste	57	0
Nguyen	55	0
Gabriel	46	1
Cindy	41	0
Ayesha	38	0
James	38	1
Ruth	36	0

See also Correlation coefficient; negative correlation; positive correlation.

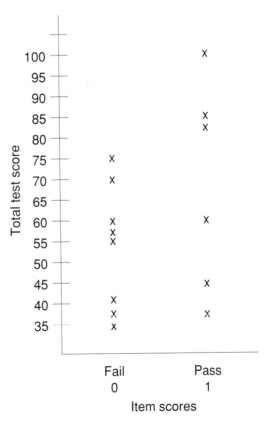

FIGURE 6.11 RELATIONSHIP BETWEEN TOTAL SCORE ON A TEST AND SCORE ON ONE PARTICULAR ITEM

Spearman Rank-Order Correlation Coefficient

Description The **Spearman rank-order correlation coefficient** is a numerical index of the degree of relationship between two quantitative variables when each variable is expressed by rankings from highest to lowest score. It is interpreted like many other correlation coefficients, that is, it varies between −1.00 and +1.00, with 0.00 indicating absence of a relationship. It is used when data are available only as rankings or when one chooses to convert scores to ranks. The latter case has the advantages and disadvantages of using a nonparametric rather than a parametric statistic. The rank-order coefficient assumes an ordinal rather than interval scale.

Example Suppose someone were interested in studying the relationship among judges' rankings on different variables at a beauty pageant. For example, the interest might be in the extent to which rankings in the swimsuit competition are correlated with those on musical talent. Ordinarily, a study of this kind probably would involve a rather large number of pageant contestants. But to keep this explanation simple, consider what the rankings might look like for only 10. Look at Table 6.3. Notice that there seems to be a relationship between the two variables. However, there are differences in how contestants ranked on the two characteristics (e.g., Lina ranked first in swimsuits but fourth in music). The Spearman correlation for these data equals .503.

See also Correlation coefficient; negative correlation; ordinal scale; positive correlation.

TABLE 6.3   Swimsuit and Musical Talent Rankings

Contestant	Swimsuit Rank	Music Rank
Lina	1	4
Lu	2	1
Felicia	3	8
Ann	4	3
Juanita	5	5
Sophie	6	2
Joan	7	10
Marilyn	8	9
Alicia	9	7
Suzy	10	6

Restricted Range Effect

Description   The **restricted range effect** is known by different names, including the *limited range problem* and the *range of talent problem*. It can cause serious difficulties in interpreting correlation coefficients. It can be especially serious when convenience samples are used.

If a population has a wide range of values on one or more of the variables involved and data actually collected from a nonrepresentative sample have a considerably narrower range, a rather large error can be made in interpreting the sample correlation coefficient. For the population (if one had the data), there may be a clear pattern of clustering about a line of best fit in the scatterplot. But if the range of the data actually analyzed reflects only part of that range, the pattern in the scatterplot for the sample may not show much clustering of plots close to a line. The actual value of the computed coefficient for the sample could be considerably different from the population—usually too low, but possibly too high in relatively rare cases.

Examples
- Suppose that a researcher wanted information on the correlation between weight and age of men in the general population between the ages of 21 and 40. Suppose also that a decision was made to use data already available on a convenience sample—in this case, the weights and ages of a group of professional football players. Because professional football players are rather homogeneous regarding both weight and age, the correlation coefficient for the two variables would be too low.
- Environmental degradation as related to number of visitors is of major concern to our National Parks. Figure 6.12 shows hypothetical data across all parks and a substantial correlation. Notice what happens if the data were obtained from only the parks with low visitation (indicated by the shaded area) or for parks with high visitation and high degradation (indicated by the cross-hatched area). In either case, the correlation would be substantially lower.

See also   Correlation coefficient; negative correlation; positive correlation; scatterplot.

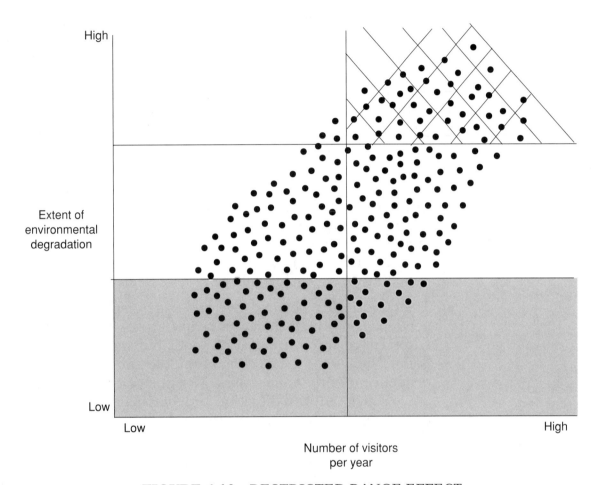

High

Extent of
environmental
degradation

Low

Low   High

Number of visitors
per year

FIGURE 6.12   RESTRICTED RANGE EFFECT

Correlation Ratio

Description The **correlation ratio** is a kind of correlation, also known as *eta squared,* that can be used to describe a curvilinear, as opposed to a straight line, relationship. The square root is eta. It is read in the same way as any other correlation coefficient, except that it cannot take negative values, that is, it varies only between 0.00 and 1.00. With a curvilinear relationship, the line of best fit to the plots in the scatterplot would be curved rather than straight.

Examples
- The relationship between task performance and anxiety level: Task performance increases as one's level of anxiety increases—up to a point. Then it decreases. Part of the line of best fit might be fairly straight, but it would start to curve at the point where performance starts to decrease.

- The relationship between age and dependence on others: Dependence on others decreases as one grows from childhood to adolescence into young adulthood, but again only up to a point. Then, with the coming of middle and old age, one's dependence on others increases. The line of best fit would first curve in a downward direction and then begin to curve upward near the middle age point, so it could not be a straight line (see Figure 6.13).

- The relationship between age and strength. Strength increases with age up to a point, but then it, too, decreases as one gets older—usually after about age 45 for most people.

See also Correlation coefficient; negative correlation; positive correlation; scatterplot.

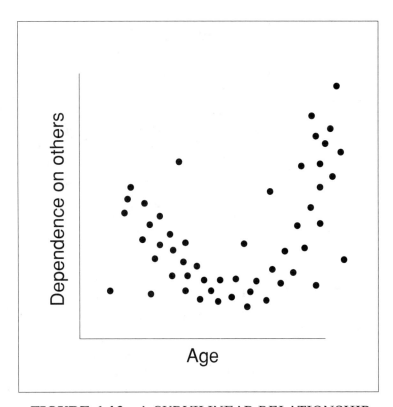

FIGURE 6.13 A CURVILINEAR RELATIONSHIP

Multiple Correlation

Description   **Multiple correlation** is a means of combining mathematically two or more variables in such a way as to maximize the correlation with another variable. The object is to measure the *combined* potential of the two or more (independent) variables for predicting values on another variable. The result is the *multiple correlation coefficient,* symbolized by the capital letter R, which has the same numerical meaning as the two-variable correlation coefficient. R^2 indicates the amount of variance in the dependent variable that can be explained by all of the independent variables taken together. Closely related is the concept of *multiple regression,* which extends the single variable regression equation to include additional predictors.

Example   It is common to find a correlation of about .60 between high school GPA and first-year college GPA. A simple regression equation can be used to predict college GPA. Adding a particular test score as another predictor variable often increases the accuracy of prediction, accompanied by an increase in the correlation with first-year college GPA to around .70.

    The overlap between high school GPA and first-year college GPA illustrates a correlation of about .60 between these variables (see Figure 6.14). Including the test score variable increases the overlap by about 13% of the college GPA circle.

See also   Correlation coefficient; negative correlation; partial correlation; positive correlation; regression; regression equation.

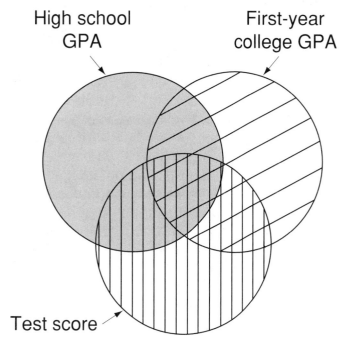

High school
GPA

First-year
college GPA

Test score

FIGURE 6.14   MULTIPLE CORRELATION

Coefficient of Determination

Description   The **coefficient of determination** indicates how much of the variation in one variable is determined or explained by another variable; more precisely, how much of the *variance* in one variable is associated with the variance in another. It is calculated by squaring the correlation coefficient, and is symbolized as r^2. Whenever two variables are consistently related, one of the variables can be used to predict the values of the second variable; hence, r^2 is very useful as an indication of the strength of association between two variables. The larger r^2 is, the more accurately predictions can be made.

The same reasoning applies in *multiple correlation*. In multiple correlation, data on *two or more* variables are used to predict values on another variable. The symbol for multiple correlation is R, and the coefficient of determination is R^2 (sometimes called the *coefficient of multiple determination*). It is interpreted in the same way as in the case of only two variables. It is the percentage of the variability in one variable that is determined or explained by two or more other variables.

Examples
- Suppose that the results of a survey show that the correlation between yearly income and amount spent annually on food by a group of senior citizens yields a coefficient of .60. The coefficient of determination would be $(.60)^2$, or .36. This means that 36% of the variation in amount spent annually on food by this group of individuals can be explained by yearly income. In other words, variation in the amount of money they spend on food is partially explained by income (but not with certainty in any causal sense).

- For the coefficient of *multiple* determination, consider the hypothetical example of a researcher investigating the extent to which the incomes of high-level executives can be predicted from their total scores on each of three psychological tests. If the multiple correlation coefficient were .55, the coefficient of multiple determination would be $(.55)^2$, or .30. This would mean that 30% of the variance in income was accounted for by the traits measured by the tests.

See also   Correlation coefficient; negative correlation; positive correlation.

a) When $r = 0$, X and Y are not related. Therefore, *none* of the variability in Y can be predicted from X; $r^2 = 0$

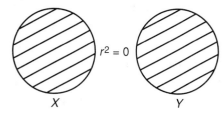

b) When $r = 0.8$, a strong relationship exists between X and Y. Therefore, the variability in Y is predicted *in part* by its relationship with X; $r^2 = .64$ (64%)

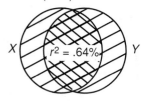

c) When $r = 1.00$, all of the variability in Y can be predicted from its relationship with X; $r^2 = 1.00$ (100%)

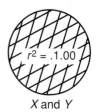

FIGURE 6.15 COEFFICIENTS OF DETERMINATION

Factor Analysis

Description   **Factor analysis** is a procedure for reducing the information originally contained in a large number of variables (or scores) into a more manageable and conceptually clearer number of variables, or *factors*. One begins by obtaining the correlations between all pairs of variables. A cluster of highly intercorrelated variables is a factor. Through an analysis that is complex mathematically, but not in practice, each of the original variables is "weighted" in terms of how strongly it correlates with each factor (from –1.00 to +1.00). The higher the weighting, the more the factor explains the variable.

Example   Suppose a researcher is interested in simplifying a number of variables that are thought to be related to male marital satisfaction at age 55. She collects the necessary data on each of 17 variables for a sample of 55-year-old married men. She carries out the factor analysis shown in Table 6.4.

These results, if real, would indicate that the information contained in the original 17 variables can be summarized with two factors. What is next required is to give meaning to these factors. Factor I could be interpreted as "affluence," because it has high weighting on "income at age 55," "parental income at time of first marriage," and other variables indicative of affluence, but it could also be interpreted as "emphasis on education" or in yet other ways. Variable I—age at first marriage—is only slightly related to (or explained by) this factor, since the weighting is –0.23. How would you interpret factors I and II?

See also   Correlation coefficient; negative correlation; positive correlation variable.

TABLE 6.4 Variables Related to Male Marital Satisfaction at Age 55

Original variables	Factor I	Factor II
1. Age at first (or only) marriage	–.23	–.55
2. Age of spouse at first (or only) marriage	–.15	–.51
3. Number of children—total	.08	.29
4. Number of male siblings	–.30	.20
5. Number of female siblings	–.25	.61
6. Number of male siblings—spouse	–.15	.65
7. Number of female siblings—spouse	–.22	.31
8. Number of years in current marriage	.31	.05
9. Income at age 25	.47	.21
10. Income at age 40	.59	.19
11. Income at age 55	.72	.10
12. Current income of spouse	.50	.23
13. Parental income at time of first marriage	.61	.10
14. Years of formal education	.51	.21
15. Years of formal education—spouse	.48	.10
16. Extent of church participation	.39	.05
17. Extent of premarital sexual experience	.01	.69

Path Analysis

Description **Path analysis** is a kind of multi-variable analysis in which possible causal relationships among several variables are represented by "path diagrams," which show the "paths" along which the suspected causal influences travel. The basic idea is to formulate a theory about the possible causes of a phenomenon (such as a person's net worth at age 40)—that is, to identify certain causal variables that might explain the phenomenon—and then to determine whether correlations among all the variables are consistent with the theory. A computer is then used to calculate path coefficients, which indicate the strength of the relationship between each of the pairs of variables in the path analysis when all the other variables are held constant. Path coefficients are standardized regression coefficients (beta weights); that is, they are regression coefficients expressed as z-scores.

Example Suppose a researcher theorizes as follows: "The income of an individual's parents directly affects the amount of education the individual receives and is also a direct cause of the person's subsequent net worth at age 40. Parental income is also a cause (negatively) of a person's accumulated loans when a student. Both education and student indebtedness are causes of the person's net worth at age 40."

How can he check this theory? The researcher must obtain measures of all four variables for a meaningful sample, calculate the intercorrelations and then proceed to the path analysis. A hypothetical outcome is illustrated in Figure 6.16, which indicates that the theory is consistent with the data and suggests the relative importance of each component. The numerical weights are interpreted similarly to correlation coefficients.

Notice that an individual's parental income affects his or her net worth at age 40 directly; it also does so indirectly, by way of its influence on the amount of a student's loan and the number of years of education he or she receives.

See also Beta weights/beta coefficient; correlation coefficient; negative correlation; positive correlation.

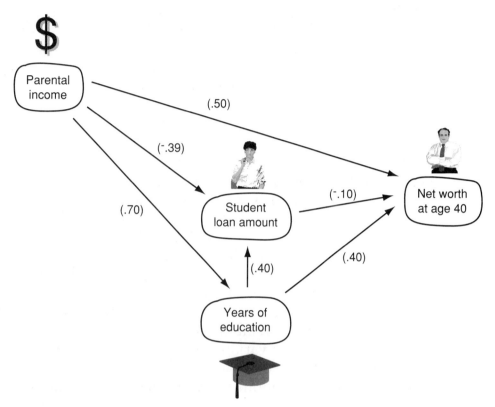

FIGURE 6.16 A PATH ANALYSIS (ARROWS INDICATE DIRECTION OF THEORETICAL CAUSATION)

Partial Correlation

Description   **Partial correlation** is a correlation between two quantitative variables after the effects of one or more other variables have been mathematically removed (controlled for or held constant). Partial correlation is symbolized r with subscripts; thus, $r_{12.3}$ means the correlation between variables 1 and 2 when variable 3 is controlled.

Example   The correlation between height and weight can be expected to be as high as .80 for a random sample of students in grades 1–12. But we know that both height and weight are greatly influenced by age. Age as a variable, therefore, can be ruled out as an effect (controlled for) by studying people who are all the same age *or* by eliminating its effect mathematically by using partial correlation. In Figure 6.17, circles A and B represent the variables of height and weight. The area of overlap between the two circles represents the correlation between these two variables. Circle C, representing the variable of age, illustrates its effect on weight and height. The use of partial correlation reduces the amount of overlap by the amount shown in the shaded area, thereby in effect eliminating the influence of age. The remaining lined area represents the degree of correlation with the effect of age removed.

See also   Correlation coefficient; correlation versus causation; multiple correlation; negative correlation; positive correlation.

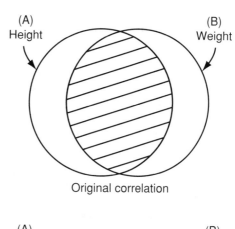

Original correlation

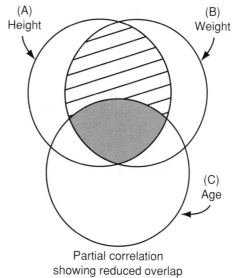

Partial correlation
showing reduced overlap

FIGURE 6.17 ELIMINATING THE EFFECTS OF AGE THROUGH PARTIAL CORRELATION

Correlation versus Causation

Description **Correlation,** the mere fact that two variables are related, does *not* necessarily mean *causation* (i.e., that one variable *causes* the other). True, many examples of correlational relationships can be found in which a change in one variable does cause an observed change in another. The correlation between eating too much and weight gain can often be correctly interpreted as a cause-and-effect relation. Overeating often does cause one to gain weight. On the other hand, just because a correlation between two variables exists does not mean there is a causal connection between the two.

Examples
- A strong positive correlation exists between the speed at which an automobile is driven and gas consumption. It is apparent that a causal connection exists between the two variables. The faster we go, the more gas must be consumed to provide enough power to overcome the air resistance.

- Some correlations may be a result of *reciprocal causal relations* between variables: Each of two variables may mutually affect the other. The relationship between workers' level of employment and the strength of the national economy is an example. When the strength of the economy increases, more people are likely to be employed. When more people are employed, there is more money for them to spend, which should increase the strength of the economy, which may, in turn, have a favorable effect on employment, and so forth. A cumulative pattern of this kind may continue for some time, at least until some third factor causes a serious decrease in employment or economic strength and possibly reverses the direction of the changes.

- Another example lies in the correlation between the levels of anger of two people arguing. If each says something that angers the other more and more, the level of anger for both people is likely to increase on a continuing basis for both.

- Because there are many examples in which a correlation is the result of a causal relationship between two variables, it is frequently assumed that whenever a correlation exists, it is *necessarily* because one of the variables caused a change in the other variable(s). This is not necessarily the case, however. Two variables can be highly correlated without either affecting the other. Any change that occurs between two correlated variables may be due to the influence of a *third* variable. For example, a study of the relationship between the number of wrinkles on a man's face and his arm strength in a group of senior citizens might very likely show that as the number of wrinkles increases, arm strength decreases. But no one would say that *wrinkles* cause the decrease in arm strength! A more likely explanation is that as one ages, the body deteriorates, that this causes *both* the increase in wrinkles and the decrease in arm strength, and that this is what accounts for the correlation.

■ Correlations can also be due to random variation, errors of measurement, or sampling error even when the true correlation coefficients for the variables involved are 0.00, especially when there are only a small number of measurements. In other words, they can be due to statistical accidents. Positive or negative correlation coefficients can often be found even in correlating different sets of numbers from a table of random numbers—which is constructed so that there can be no such (long run) relationships. Each of the three tables shown below contains pairs of numbers chosen from a table of random numbers. The correlation coefficients are shown at the bottom of each table.

TABLE 6.5 Pairs of Numbers Selected from a Table of Random Numbers: I		TABLE 6.6 Pairs of Numbers Selected from a Table of Random Numbers: II		TABLE 6.7 Pairs of Numbers Selected from a Table of Random Numbers: III	
X	Y	X	Y	X	Y
3	6	6	6	1	9
4	3	8	6	8	2
3	2	1	7	4	2
1	6	9	9	8	4
0	3	3	3	2	5
5	5	0	1	2	2
0	5	4	0	3	8
3	2	5	9	6	6
7	8	8	1	5	4
7	4	1	2	3	2
$r = .264$		$r = .383$		$r = -.342$	

■ Notice that, although all of the X and Y numbers in Figures 6.5–6.7 were selected strictly at random, the resulting correlation coefficients are considerably different from the expected value of 0.00 (since there is no long-run relation between these pairs of scores). This example provides support for the assertion that a correlation coefficient (either positive or negative) can result from chance if the sample is small enough.

See also Experiment; negative correlation; positive correlation.

Set 7

Regression analysis is essentially an extension of correlation among quantitative variables. If a relationship exists between two (or more) variables, information on one variable can be used to predict the value(s) of the other(s). Regression concepts are concerned with the rationale and techniques of prediction.

Relationships between Quantitative Variables: Regression

Regression

Description   The term **regression** refers to any of several methods concerned with making predictions about some variables based on knowing other variables. Regression techniques are used to answer questions such as "How well can I predict the values of one variable, such as weight (Y), by knowing the values for another variable, such as height (X)?

Examples ■   Tall people, in general, tend to weigh more than short people, although there are exceptions. (You probably know someone who is very tall but doesn't weigh a lot.) Let's consider the heights and weights of a group of bicyclists (see Table 7.1).

     We have intentionally listed these men in order of their heights. Notice that the taller men also tend to weigh more, although the trend is not perfect (some of the shorter men weigh more than some of the taller ones). When such a linear relationship exists, regression methods can be used to predict the weight of a man who is not in the group, if we know his height. Similarly, we could predict a man's height if his weight is known.

TABLE 7.1   Heights and Weights of a Group of 14 Bicyclists

Name	Height in Inches	Weight in Pounds
Saul	80	214
Mac	75	190
Jim	71	247
Dennis	69	186
Rafael	68	160
Eugene	68	175
Hiro	66	140
Richard	65	123
Paul	65	136
Gordon	64	121
Ali	62	114
Walter	60	155
Robert	59	118
Tyrell	57	120

■ An agricultural researcher wants to find out whether there is a relationship between use of a chemical fertilizer and the amount of growth of carrot plants. He plants carrot seeds in 10 separate pots and systematically varies the amount of fertilizer given to the different plants. Other important factors, such as the amount of watering, are kept the same for all plants. At the end of the growing season, the carrots are pulled up, and their roots are measured. The amount of fertilizer given to each plant at each weekly feeding, and the results of the experiment, are shown in Figure 7.1.

Notice that the top ends of the carrots are nearly in a straight line, which has been drawn as close as possible to the tops of the carrots. We now can use the slanted line to predict the length of carrots when a selected amount of fertilizer is used. For example, find the 1.5 cc point on the horizontal baseline (it's halfway between carrot 8 and carrot 9). Follow the dotted line from that point up to the slanted line, and then across to the vertical axis. This indicates a carrot length of 7 inches. Seven inches, therefore, would be our approximate prediction of carrot length when 1.5 cc of the fertilizer is used weekly.

See also Intercept; negative correlation; positive correlation; regression equation; regression line; slope.

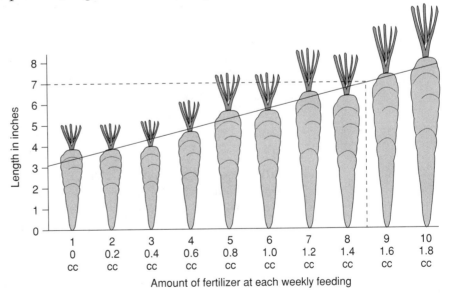

FIGURE 7.1 PREDICTING THE SIZE OF CARROTS BASED ON THE AMOUNT OF FERTILIZER USED WEEKLY

Regression Equation

Description A **regression equation** (also called "prediction equation")is an algebraic equation that expresses the relationship between two or more variables. The regression equation is usually written $Y' = a + bX$. Y is the dependent (or predicted) variable; X is the *independent* (or predictor) variable; b is the *slope* of the regression line; and a is the *intercept*. With more than one predictor, the equation is as follows (using three predictors as an example): $Y' = a + b_1X_1 + b_2X_2 + b_3X_3$, where X_1, X_2, and X_3 are scores on three predictor variables.

Examples
- In a study of the relationship between education and income, a researcher finds that (1) people with only a grade school education have an income of $12,000 a year and (2) each year of education adds an additional $5000 to a person's annual income, so people with a four-year college education have an annual income of $52,000 a year. This would yield the following regression equation: Annual income = $12,000 + 5000 × the number of years of education. $Y' = 12,000 + 5X$, where Y' equals predicted annual income and X equals numbers of years of education.

- Regression equations are used in making predictions, such as predicting the combined weight of a truck and its load on the basis of the number of boxes in the load, each box weighing exactly the same amount (see Figure 7.2). Y' is the predicted value (the weight of the truck after being loaded). Suppose that the unloaded truck weighs 3219 lb and that each of the boxes weighs 100 lb. The regression equation would be $Y' = 3219 + 100X$, where Y' equals the weight of the truck loaded and X equals the number of boxes.

- The regression equation for predicting G.P.A. at a particular university from a combination of high school G.P.A. (X_1), SAT verbal scores (X_2), and SAT mathematical scores (X_3) might look like the following:

$$Y' = .22 + .59X_1 + .0008X_2 + .0004X_3$$

See also Intercept; regression; slope.

$Y' = 3219 + 1(100) = 3319$ lb $Y' = 3219 + 6(100) = 3819$ lb

FIGURE 7.2   USING A REGRESSION EQUATION TO PREDICT
WEIGHT OF A TRUCK AND ITS LOAD

Beta Weights/Beta Coefficient

Description The formula for *multiple regression* (three predictor variables) is $Y' = a + b_1X_1 + b_2X_2 + b_3X_3$, where X_1, X_2, and X_3 are scores on the three predictors. If this equation is expressed in *standard scores* (*z*-scores), a becomes 0 and each b becomes β. The equation is then

$$z_y^1 = \beta_1 z_1 + \beta_2 z_2 + \beta_3 z_3.$$

Each β is what is known as a **beta weight,** which is numerically different from b. This is because the change to standard scores mathematically changes the constants in the equation. Comparing β weights (not b's!) shows the relative contribution (or weight) of each predictor variable.

Example If amount of vegetation on a pasture is predicted from (1) the amount of rainfall, (2) number of cattle grazing it, and (3) the length of the grazing period, the equation might be

$$z_{veg} = .52z_1 - .04z_2 - .24z_3.$$

If this were the outcome, rainfall would be shown to have more than twice the influence of duration of grazing and 13 times the impact of number of cattle.

See also Regression; regression equation.

FIGURE 7.3   BETA WEIGHTS

Regression Line

Description A **regression line** is a graphic picture of a regression equation. It is the line drawn through the pattern of points in a scatterplot that best summarizes the relationship between the two variables represented in the scatterplot. When the regression line slopes upward (from left to right), this indicates a positive relationship; when it slopes downward (from left to right), this indicates a negative relationship.

Example A high school history teacher notices that those students who check out a lot of books from the library tend to get higher grades on the monthly history tests than do the students who check out only a few books. She wants to set up some way of predicting (approximately) a student's history test score once she knows how many books the student checks out. She collects data on 12 students (see Table 7.2) and then plots the data.

TABLE 7.2 Relationship between Number of Library Books Checked Out by a Group of 25 Students and Their History Test Scores

Student	Average Number of Books Checked Out Weekly (X)	History Test Scores (Y)
Josh	1	10
Alicia	2	30
Mahdu	3	20
Ramon	4	40
Jack	5	60
Linda	5	20
LeAnn	6	60
Sara	7	50
Felix	7	70
Tony	8	50
Tom	8	70
Lana	9	90

See also Regression; regression equation.

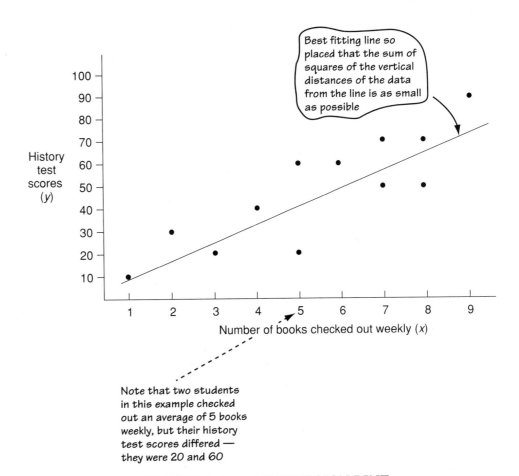

FIGURE 7.4   A REGRESSION LINE

Slope/Intercept

Description   **Slope** is the rate at which a line or curve rises or falls over a given horizontal distance. Slope most commonly refers to the steepness of a *regression line* and is usually symbolized by the letter b in a regression equation. The slope of a line is calculated by taking any two points on the line and dividing the vertical distance (known as the *rise*) by the horizontal distance between them (known as the *run*). The **intercept** is the point at which a regression line crosses (i.e., intercepts) the vertical (y) axis. It is the spot where the value on the horizontal axis is zero.

Examples
- In a positive relationship between children's ages and their weight, for example, a regression line for the scatterplot would slope upward from left to right.

- In a negative relationship, such as amount of rainfall and the danger of a fire in a forest, the regression line for the scatterplot would slope downward from left to right.

- When the correlation coefficient for the relationship between two variables is zero, the regression line is parallel to the horizontal axis of the scatterplot, and the numerical value of the slope is zero. This is because the *rise* mentioned above is also zero, making the result when the rise is divided by the run zero as well.

- If we were to graph the correlation between life expectancy of a group of individuals (the dependent variable) and amount of exercise of members of the same group (the independent variable), the regression line that would best summarize the data might look like that shown in Figure 7.6. People who do not exercise at all would have a life expectancy of 60 years according to these (hypothetical) data; 60 is the intercept, that is, it is the expected value when the score on the independent variable is zero.

See also   Intercept; regression; regression equation; regression line.

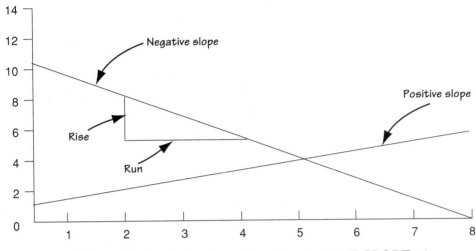

FIGURE 7.5 POSITIVE AND NEGATIVE SLOPE

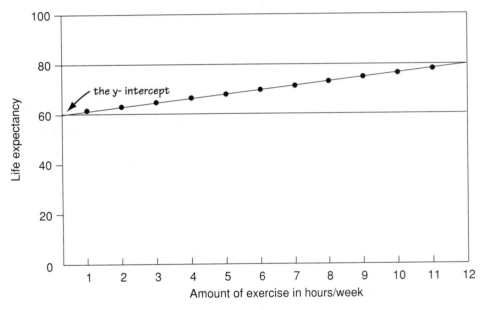

FIGURE 7.6 THE *y*-INTERCEPT

Least Squares Criterion (or Principle)

Description   The **least squares criterion** is a criterion used to determine which, of several, possible estimates of a score on a dependent variable from a *known* score on an independent variable is most valid. There are many possible regression lines that can be drawn with a given set of points in a scatterplot. Similarly, there are several possible measures of central tendency that can be used to summarize a distribution of scores. The least squares criterion is a rule for choosing a statistic so that the sum of the squared deviations from it is minimized.

Examples
- In regression analysis, we want to draw the regression line so that the accuracy of prediction using the regression line is maximized. Prediction accuracy is best when the regression line is drawn using the least squares criterion (as in part A of Figure 7.7) than when any other equation is used to draw the regression line (as in part B of Figure 7.7).

- The mean is the least squares estimate of central tendency. The sum of the squares of all the score deviations from the mean is less than from any other value, such as the median or the mode. In Table 7.3, the sum of the d^2 values = 178, which is a smaller sum of squares than for any other value between 7 and 22.

TABLE 7.3   Using the Mean as the Least Squares Criterion

Scores	d	d^2
22	+8	64
19	+5	25
17	+3	9
13	−1	1
13	−1	1
12	−2	4
9	−5	25
7	−7	49
Mean = 14		178

Legend: d=deviation of score from the mean.

See also   Mean; regression line.

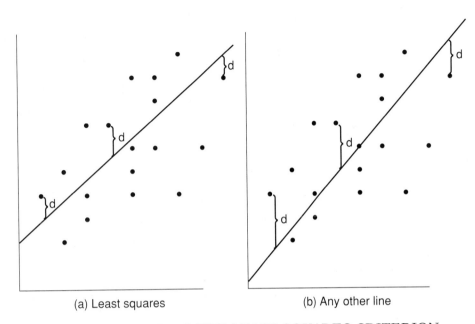

(a) Least squares   (b) Any other line

FIGURE 7.7   USING THE LEAST SQUARES CRITERION

Standard Error of Estimate

Description The **standard error of estimate** is a number showing the extent to which a predicted score or measurement is likely to be in error. Such errors are called *errors of prediction* and are inevitable in all practical prediction. The larger the standard error of estimate, the less accurate the predictions. While an estimate of error for curvilinear regression (based on curvilinear relationships) is possible, in practice most error estimation is based on linear or straight-line regression. The standard error for a given set of data is based on the discrepancies between the actual scores for each individual and the scores predicted from the regression line (and/or the regression equation). It is the *standard deviation* of all such discrepancies.

Example Figure 7.8 presents a hypothetical relationship between scores on a test of manual dexterity and subsequent on-the-job productivity in a tool-and-die factory. All individuals scoring an A on the test will be predicted to have productivity scores at B. However, those with different test scores show discrepancies of varying degrees from predicted productivity. Person P shows a small discrepancy (d_1) from that predicted from the regression line; Person O, a larger discrepancy (d_2). The standard error of estimate is based on a combination of all such discrepancies and is the best estimate to be applied to each future prediction.

See also Regression; regression equation; regression line; slope; scatterplot; standard deviation.

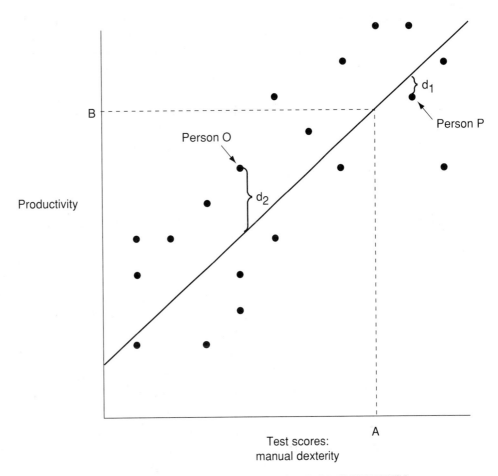

FIGURE 7.8 PREDICTING PRODUCTIVITY

Discriminant Function Analysis

Description **Discriminant function analysis** is a way of indicating which of several groups (of people, objects, etc.) a particular individual is "most like" on the basis of a combination of measurements. The measurements are mathematically weighted to ensure the fewest number of mistakes in predicting group membership. Conceptually and mathematically, the procedure is similar to multiple regression, except that the outcome is a predicted group, rather than a predicted score.

Examples

- Suppose a student can't decide whether she wants to study to be a veterinarian, a nurse, or a pharmacist. If a college has measurements on a sufficient number of individuals enrolled in each program and an advisor has the same measurements for her, discriminant function analysis can be used to predict which of the three groups of students she is most similar to. This does not, of course, mean that she ought to make the indicated choice, but it may help her to decide.

- Anthropologists, botanists, and other scientists sometimes have difficulty determining the best classification for a particular fossil, plant, or other specimen. If a variety of measurements are available for members of known classifications and for the new specimen, discriminant function analysis can help in the classification.

- A young attorney is trying to decide whether he is best suited to work as a defense or prosecution lawyer. Comparing his scores on three different measures with those of samples of practicing defense attorneys and prosecutors gives the results shown in Figure 7.9. As you can see, it is hard to determine which group he is most like. Discriminant function analysis would provide a mathematical solution to his dilemma.

See also Regression.

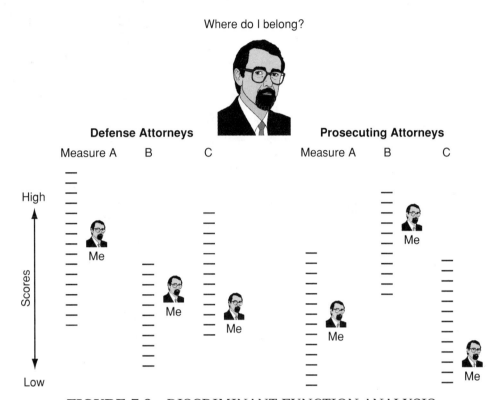

FIGURE 7.9 DISCRIMINANT FUNCTION ANALYSIS

Set 8

Often, data exist in categorical rather than quantitative form. The question is whether being a member of a particular category (e.g., male) means that it is likely that the individual is a member of a particular category on another variable (e.g., Republican). This section presents concepts that are applicable to this topic.

Relationships between Categorical Variables

Categorical Variable

Description A **categorical variable** is a variable that is made up of distinct, separate units or categories. Even though they are sometimes expressed in numbers, these numbers only identify the category or group to which an individual belongs. Categorical variables indicate *type* or *kind* (as gender does by categorizing people as male or female), but they do not indicate differences in *amount*. Categorical variables are also called *nominal* or *qualitative* variables.

Examples
- Suits in a deck of cards (hearts, spades, clubs, diamonds)
- Using the numbers 1, 2, 3, and 4 to identify individuals as single, married, divorced, or separated. Note that these categories do not reflect amounts of anything; they reflect only the group to which different individuals belong. The number of individuals in each category, of course, can be counted.
- Describing individuals in terms of the kind of sport they prefer (basketball fan, tennis player, golf enthusiast, etc.).
- Ethnic origin (Native American, African American, Hispanic, Polynesian, Latino, Chinese, Japanese, and so forth).

See also Continuous variable; nominal scale; qualitative variable; quantitative variable.

Variable: *categories* of different *types* of aircraft

Variable: *categories* of different *types* of animals

Variable: *categories* of different *types* of trees

Variable: *categories* of different *types* of vehicles

FIGURE 8.1   CATEGORICAL VARIABLES

Numbers and Categorical Variables

Description   Confusion often occurs because of the way numbers are used with categorical variables. A number is often assigned to each category for ease of analysis—particularly when using a computer. When used this way, the numbers do not indicate differences in amount. If males are assigned the number "1" and females the number "2," for example, there is no implication that females are more of something than males. The other way that numbers are used with categorical variables is to indicate the count within each category. Thus, for a particular group, we might find that there are 40 in the male category and 50 in the female category.

Examples

1. Categorical variable:

	1		2
Handedness	Left-handed	vs.	Right-handed
N=	(60)		(230)

2. Categorical variable:

	1	2	3	4	5
Ethnicity	Black	Latino	Asian	Caucasian	Other
N=	(380)	(520)	(240)	(780)	(120)

3. Categorical variable:

	1	2	3
Political Party	Democrat	Republican	Independent
N=	(1600)	(1400)	(500)

See also   Categorical variable.

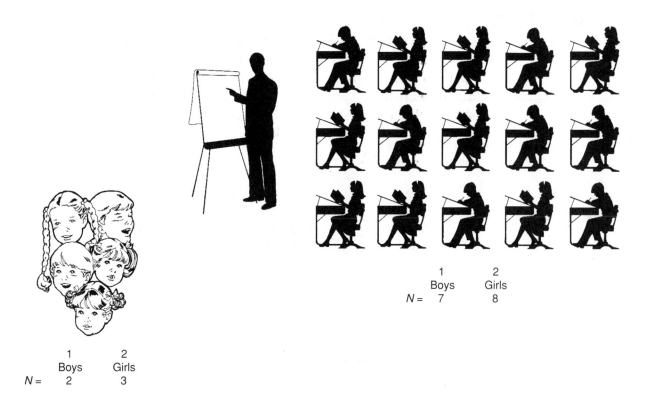

FIGURE 8.2   COUNTING CATEGORICAL VARIABLES

Crossbreak Table

Description A **crossbreak table** (sometimes called a *contingency table,* or a *cross-tabulation*) is used to display relationships or patterns for two categorical variables. They may be either "true" categorical variables, or variables that are categorized either for convenience or to facilitate measurement. Combinations of categories are shown together with the frequencies occurring in each combination. The data in crossbreak tables are commonly analyzed by a *chi-square* analysis.

Examples
- A crossbreak table that presents the relationship between gender and political party affiliation for a sample of 1000 adults in a senior citizen's center, as shown in Table 8.1 (true categories).
- A crossbreak table that presents the relationship between type of illness (true categories) and geographic area (convenient categories) for a sample of 1200 incidents reported during a six-month period (see Table 8.2).
- A crossbreak table that presents the relationship between attitude toward welfare and a belief in human goodness, for a sample of 800 teenagers attending a Christian Fellowship weekend, as shown in Table 8.3 (convenience categories).
- A crossbreak table that presents the relationship between level of customer service and type of retail store, for a sample of shoppers in Detroit, MI.

See also Chi-square test.

TABLE 8.1 Relationship between Gender and Political Party Affiliation

	Male	Female	Total
Democrat	200	230	430
Republican	260	200	460
Other	40	70	110
Total	500	500	1000

TABLE 8.2 Relationship between Type of Illness and Geographic Area of Occurrence

	Illness			
	Pneumonia	Allergy	Skin Cancer	Total
Northeast	150	110	55	315
Northwest	130	100	55	285
Southeast	70	110	130	310
Southwest	50	80	160	290
Total	400	400	400	1200

TABLE 8.3 Relationship between Attitude toward Welfare and a Belief in Human Goodness

	Basically Good	Basically Bad	Don't Know	Totals
Maintain welfare	200	80	120	400
Decrease welfare	160	200	40	400
Total	360	280	160	800

Degrees of Freedom

Description **Degrees of freedom,** usually abbreviated as d.f., are the number of values that are free to vary (take on any number) in computing a statistic. Degrees of freedom are required when computing and/or evaluating statistics such as an "F ratio," a "chi-square," or a "t-test." While difficult to grasp conceptually, straightforward rules make degrees of freedom easy to determine in practice.

Examples
- Any set of numbers initially has as many degrees of freedom as there are numbers in the set. For example, there are many sets of three single-digit numbers—(2, 6, 9); (3, 2, 0); (1, 4, 7), etc. All of the numbers in each set are free to vary so there are 3 d.f. Once we know what one of the numbers in the set is, however, that number can no longer vary, and hence one degree of freedom is lost and 2 remain. In other words, all but one of the numbers are free to vary. Once we know two of the three numbers, two d.f. are lost, one is left—unless we have specified what the total must be (e.g., 10). In that case, once two numbers are known, the third is determined and no d.f. remain. For example, if two of the numbers in a set of three that must add up to 10 are 4 and 1, the third number *must* be 5; if two of the numbers in another set that adds up to 10 are 0 and 1, the third number must be 9, and so forth.

- Any set of numbers in which changes can be made initially has as many degrees of freedom as there are numbers in the set. When a mean is calculated, one degree of freedom is lost because, to fit the calculated mean, all but *one* of the numbers can vary, since the last number can always generate the same mean; for example, the mean of 20, 24, and 31 is 25. Once we determine the mean, two of the numbers can vary, but the third cannot. Thus, if the first two numbers are 40 and 55, the third must be –20 in order for the mean to be 25.

- A 3×2 crossbreak table with six cells has two degrees of freedom. Why? Because, once the marginal totals are known, knowing the frequency in any two cells determines the rest. Thus, once we know the values of X and Y in the table, the rest are fixed—they cannot vary (see Table 8.4).

See also Chi-square test; crossbreak table.

TABLE 8.4   Degrees of Freedom in a 3 × 2 Table

	A	B	C	Totals
1	X			60
		Y		40
2	30	30	40	100

FIGURE 8.3   DEGREES OF FREEDOM

Chi-Square Test

Description The **chi-square test** is used to determine the likelihood or probability that an observed relationship between two or more categorical variables is statistically significant (i.e., not due to chance). The best known use of the chi-square test is when one wishes to determine whether there are statistically significant differences between the observed (i.e., actual) frequencies and the expected frequencies of two variables presented in a *crossbreak table*. The larger the differences between the obtained and expected frequencies, the greater is the likelihood that the difference is not due to chance.

As with all inference procedures, the chi-square test produces a value (χ^2), which can then be looked up in the appropriate table to see whether it is statistically significant.

Examples
- Suppose a market researcher wants to determine whether male and female TV viewers differ in their preference for different kinds of television programs. She finds that the males indicate a preference for sports and action programs, whereas the females say that they prefer news and comedy shows. She then uses a chi-square test to assess whether these differences represent something more than just chance (i.e., are statistically significant), and finds that they do (see Table 8.5).

- What, if anything, is the relationship between religious preference and economic orientation in the United States? Suppose an economist randomly selects a sample of 1000 individuals and finds out their religious preference. He then asks them what economic system they identify with. He concludes that Protestants are more likely to identify with capitalism and agnostics with socialism but that no clear pattern identifies itself for the other religious preferences. He then uses a chi-square test to assess whether this pattern is due to something more than just chance.

See also Crossbreak table; degrees of freedom.

TABLE 8.5 Relationship between Gender of Viewer and Type of Television Show Preferred

	Sports	Action	News	Comedy	Nature	Total
Men	90	70	50	40	50	300
Women	40	50	80	80	50	300
Total	130	120	130	120	100	600

chi-square = 42.82, with 4 degrees of freedom

$p < .001$

Contingency Coefficient: C

Description The **contingency coefficient** is a measure of the relationship existing between categorical variables. It is based on the *chi-square test* and is symbolized by the capital letter C. Calculation of C is extremely easy once the chi-square statistic has been determined. The formula is:

$$C = \sqrt{\frac{\text{chi-square}}{N + \text{chi-square}}}$$

Unfortunately, interpretation of C is not so straightforward; it can vary upward from .00, but the maximum upper limit depends on the size of the crossbreak table. As examples, the upper limit for a 2×2 table is .71; for a 3×3 table, it is .81; for a 4×4 table, it is .86. For a $K \times K$ table, the upper limit is

$$\sqrt{\frac{K - 1}{K}}.$$

For unequal-sized tables, such as a 3×4 table, upper limits are unknown but can be estimated. Since upper limits vary, the same value of C indicates a different degree of relationship for different sized tables, although as with other correlation coefficients, the higher the coefficient in a particular sized table, the stronger the relationship.

Example A researcher wonders whether there is a relationship between the level of service provided by different kinds of retail stores. He obtains the data shown in Table 8.6, and calculates the chi-square statistic. For these data, $C = .38$ which, when compared to the possible range of .00 to .81 (for a 3×3 table) indicates a moderate relationship.

See also Chi-square test; crossbreak table.

TABLE 8.6   Relationship between Level of Service Provided and Type of Retail Store

Service Level	Chain	Franchise	Locally Owned	Total
High	40	85	150	275
Moderate	80	100	70	250
Low	140	75	40	255
Total	260	260	260	780

$$C = .38$$

Simpson's Paradox

Description   **Simpson's Paradox** is simply this: the nature of an observed relationship between two categorical variables can change markedly when the data from several groups are combined into just one group. Sometimes the relationship even changes direction.

Example   Suppose that two hospitals participate in an experiment to test a new drug for prostate cancer. Jamestown Hospital is a major research center, famous for study of this disease. Brown Hospital is a small hospital in a comparatively remote area of the country.

Both hospitals agree to include 600 subjects in the study. At Jamestown Hospital, 500 patients are randomly assigned to be given the new drug; the remaining 100 will get an older, more traditionally used drug. The staff at Brown Hospital, a bit uncomfortable with using an experimental drug on so many patients, randomly assigns only 100 patients to be given the new drug; the remaining 500 are given the more traditional drug. The survival rates are shown in Table 8.7.

When the data are analyzed separately for the two hospitals, it is clear that the new drug is an improvement on the older, traditionally used drug. The risk of dying when given the older drug is greater at both hospitals (see Table 8.8).

The researchers now combine all of the data so that they can estimate the overall reduction in risk at both hospitals combined when patients are given the new drug. These data are shown in Table 8.9.

Oops! What happened? It now looks as though the older drug is better than the new one. The problem is that the more advanced cases of the cancer were treated at Jamestown. As a result, more of these patients died. And *because* they went to Jamestown, they were more likely to get the new drug! When the results from both hospitals are combined, we lose this important information, and the resulting interpretation is incorrect.

See also   Confounding; crossbreak table; extraneous variable.

TABLE 8.7   Survival Rates for Two Drugs at Two Hospitals

	Jamestown Hospital			Brown Hospital		
	Survive	**Die**	**Total**	**Survive**	**Die**	**Total**
Old drug	5	95	100	250	250	500
New drug	50	450	500	95	5	100
Total	55	545	600	345	255	600

TABLE 8.8   Risk Compared for Old and New Drugs

	Jamestown Hospital	Brown Hospital
Risk of dying: old drug	95/100 = .95	250/500 = .50
Risk of dying: new drug	450/500 = .90	5/100 = .05
Relative risk	.95/.90 = 1.06	.50/.05 = 10.0

TABLE 8.9   Estimating Overall Risk Reduction from Using Two Different Drugs for Prostate Cancer

	Survive	**Die**	**Total**	**Risk of Death**
Old drug	255	345	600	345/600 = .58
New drug	145	455	600	455/600 = .76
Total	400	800	1200	

Probability is concerned with the likelihood that particular events will occur. Some events (e.g., the sun rising today) are intuitively more likely than others (e.g., an earthquake today). The concepts presented in this section help us to be more precise in our expectations. Probability is also crucial to an understanding of a major topic in statistics: inferential reasoning.

Probability

Listed Sequentially

probability
p value
theoretical probability
empirical (actual) probability
subjective probability
independence
mutually exclusive outcomes
Gambler's Fallacy
probability rules
binomial distribution
odds
odds ratio

Listed Alphabetically

binomial distribution
empirical (actual) probability
Gambler's Fallacy
independence
mutually exclusive outcomes
odds
odds ratio
p value
probability
probability rules
subjective probability
theoretical probability

Probability

Description   A statement of **probability** is an assertion about how likely it is that a particular event or relationship will occur. More precisely, it is the expectation that a given outcome will happen out of all possible outcomes. *Levels of probability* are expressed in terms of numbers ranging from .00 to 1.00. A probability of .00 is a prediction that an event will *not* occur. A probability of 1.00 is a prediction that an event is *certain* to occur. Levels between .00 and 1.00 are for predictions ranging from very unlikely to almost (but not quite) certain.

Examples
- The probability that someone will draw a spade from an honest deck of playing cards is 13/52, or .25 (there are 52 cards in the deck, 13 of which are spades). The probability of drawing a black card is 26/52, or .50 (half of the cards in the deck are black, and half are red). The probability of drawing an ace is 4/52, or .077.
- The probability that a newborn child will be a boy is about .51.
- Two dice are thrown. The probability of getting a total of 4 spots is 3/36, or .083 (see Figure 9.1).

See also   Conditional probability; empirical probability; joint probability; subjective probability; theoretical probability.

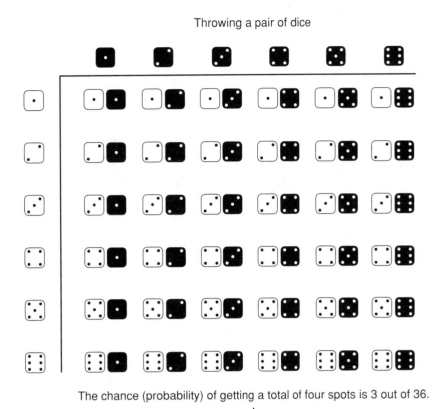

Throwing a pair of dice

The chance (probability) of getting a total of four spots is 3 out of 36.

FIGURE 9.1   WHAT'S THE CHANCE OF GETTING A 4?

p Value

Description   The small, italicized letter *p* in the term **p value** is short for *probability value*. It is commonly found in an expression such as $p < .05$. This expression means that the probability (p) that a particular obtained result was due to chance is less than (<) 5% (.05). The smaller the *p* value, the greater is the likelihood that the obtained result is *not* due simply to chance. The *p* value (.05, .01, etc.) is the actual likelihood (probability) of an obtained statistical result. It is then compared with the *alpha level* (also .05, .01, etc.) specified beforehand by the researcher to decide whether it (p) is statistically significant.

Examples
- When $p < .01$, this means that the odds are 99 to 1 *against* the obtained result being due merely to chance—that is, being a fluke.
- When $p < .05$, the odds are 19 to 1 against the obtained result being due merely to chance. What would $p < .001$ mean?
- When $p < .10$, the odds are 9 to 1 against the result being due merely to chance. Results with *p* values this large, however, are seldom considered statistically significant.

See also   Alpha level; probability; statistical significance.

FIGURE 9.2 *p* VALUE

Theoretical Probability

Description   **Theoretical probability** is the likelihood of an event occurring as deduced from a theory or model, rather than from observation or experience. This type of probability involves determining the chance *in the long run* (i.e., after a great many trials) of an event occurring.

Examples
- Examples of theoretical probability include predicting the outcomes of tossing a coin, rolling a die, or drawing a card out of an honest deck of 52 playing cards over the long run. The level of probability can be predicted, without collecting any data, by reasoning based on the nature of the coin and what happens when it is tossed, on the number of sides on a die, or on how many cards there are of each kind in a deck.
- In tossing a penny, the long run probability of getting a head is very close to .5. To test this, the English mathematician John Kerrick, while a prisoner of the Germans during World War II, tossed a coin a total of 10,000 times. Heads came up a total of 5067 times (50.67% of the time).
- If the number of people who buy raffle tickets is known (7), the theoretical probability of any one ticket winning the raffle is $1/n$.
- The theoretical probability of an individual being born on any particular day of the week is 1/7.

See also   Probability.

FIGURE 9.3 THEORETICAL PROBABILITY

Empirical (Actual) Probability

Description **Empirical probability** refers to a count of the number of events of a particular type that have *actually* occurred, divided by the total number of possible events of this type that could have occurred. This type of probability can be determined only after making some observations or conducting an experiment. Empirical probability describes what actually happened; it is usually contrasted with theoretical probability.

Example An example of empirical probability appeared in the August 1, 1995, *San Francisco Chronicle*. Research was reported on the hormone leptin, which acts as a "thermostat" in controlling the retention and reduction of fat in mice. (The results may have implications for weight control in humans because humans produce a hormone that is almost identical to the leptin in mice.) The probability of losing weight through the use of leptin could be determined by dividing the number of mice that lost weight by the total number of mice who were injected with leptin. Thus, if the researchers find that 53 out of the 57 mice that were injected lose weight, the empirical probability (describing what really happened) would be .930, that is, 53/57 = .930. Note that this probability applies only in this particular study.

See also Conditional probability; probability; theoretical probability.

FIGURE 9.4 THREE DIFFERENT KINDS OF PROBABILITY

Subjective Probability

Description   **Subjective probability** is an individual's own personal belief about the chance of something happening. This should not be decided on haphazardly, however. In any serious determination of subjective probability, the person involved considers all of the factors that are related in one way or another to the chance that the event will occur. Subjective probability is a fundamental part of an important branch of statistics known as Bayesian statistics. It involves making an estimate as to the likelihood of something happening and then revising this estimate as more and more evidence becomes available.

Example   When a parent considers whether to allow a child to walk a few blocks to and from school, neither the theoretical nor the empirical approach to probability is appropriate. No theory or mathematical model is available that a parent can apply. No systematically obtained data are likely to be available (regarding the risks involved in having the child take a particular route) that the parent might use for analysis. It boils down to the parent's own personal estimate of the likelihood that any harm will come to the child in walking to and from school. (See Figure 9.5).

See also   Empirical probability; probability; theoretical probability.

FIGURE 9.5 SUBJECTIVE PROBABILITY

Independence

Description **Independence** is the opposite of dependence. If two variables, or sets of data, are independent, knowing the value of one provides no information about the value of the other. It also means that the occurrence of one event does not change the likelihood of another event occurring. In short, when one event does not depend on another, it is an *independent* event. There is no cause-and-effect relationship between the two.

Examples

■ The number of cars going past a chosen point on a particular street in Rotorua, New Zealand, each day for a 90-day period would likely be independent of the value of a share of stock at the end of each day of trading for the same 90 days on the New York Stock Exchange.

■ It would be reasonable to conclude that the number on a lottery ticket that a person purchased was independent of whether he was wearing his "lucky" hat.

■ The outcome of the spin of an honest roulette wheel (i.e., whether the ball lands in a red, black, or green slot) provides no information about what the outcome of the next spin will be. Each spin of the wheel is independent of any other, because the wheel doesn't remember where it stopped on previous spins (unless, of course, the wheel is rigged).

■ Picking a second card at random from a new deck of 52 playing cards, after the first card picked has been replaced in the deck (and the deck is then reshuffled), is independent of which card was picked first.

■ Knowing that the first child born in a given year is a boy is independent of what gender the second child born that year will be.

See also Gambler's fallacy; sampling with replacement.

FIGURE 9.6 YOU'VE GOT ABOUT A 50–50 CHANCE OF HAVING ANOTHER GIRL!

Mutually Exclusive Outcomes

Description   A **mutually exclusive outcome** (or event) occurs when one outcome precludes the occurrence of another outcome. Mutually exclusive outcomes cannot occur simultaneously. The probability that they will occur together is zero.

Examples
- When you roll a die only once, it is impossible to roll both a 3 and a 5. One precludes the other.
- If you select one card from a complete deck of 52 playing cards, it cannot be both a spade and a heart.
- If you purchase a new car, it cannot be both a Cadillac and a Lincoln. The car can be one make or the other, but it cannot be both.
- The marital status of *legally married* and that of *single* are mutually exclusive. You can be one or the other, but not both.

See also   Independence.

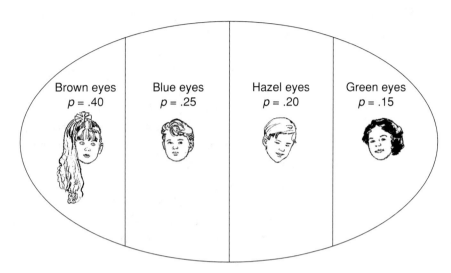

Probability of having both blue eyes *and* brown eyes is zero.

FIGURE 9.7 MUTUALLY EXCLUSIVE OUTCOMES

Gambler's Fallacy

Description The **Gambler's Fallacy** is a common mistake that many inexperienced gamblers make: treating independent events as though they were dependent.

Failure to understand the concept of independence often leads neophyte gamblers to believe that after several losses, they are bound to win. The longer the string of losses in betting on ball games, on the horses, at the craps table, when playing blackjack, and so forth, the more convinced these individuals become that they are "bound to win" soon. Accordingly, they increase their bet, but alas, they continue to lose! Why? Because their reasoning is flawed. The odds in gambling do not change simply because a person has had several losses in a row. Similarly, having several wins in a row does *not* mean that a person will keep on winning.

Examples:

- The most familiar example is that of tossing a fair coin. If a person concludes, after tossing five heads in a row, that the next toss is more likely to be a tail, he or she would be committing the Gambler's Fallacy. The person would be assuming that the sixth toss was dependent on the previous five, when actually each toss is independent of the other tosses. (See Figure 9.8.)

- Suppose you thoroughly shuffle a deck of previously unopened playing cards and then draw one card at random from the deck. It is a red card (a heart or diamond). You replace the card, shuffle the deck thoroughly again, and pick another card at random. It, too, is red. You do this a third, a fourth, and a fifth time, each time replacing the card into the deck. Each time, you draw a red card. You are committing the Gambler's Fallacy if you believe that the sixth card to be drawn is more likely to be black (a spade or club). Because you replaced the drawn card each time, each subsequent draw was independent of the others. On the other hand, if you do *not* replace the red card each time, this would make drawing a black card on subsequent draws slightly more likely. Can you see why?

See also Independence; probability; sampling with replacement.

FIGURE 9.8 THE GAMBLER'S FALLACY

Probability Rules

Description   **Probability rules** are some basic, simple (and quite logical) rules that apply to how probabilities relate to each other and to actual events. An impossible event, for example, has a probability of zero, while an event that is certain to happen has a probability of 1. Here are some other rules:

> *Rule One:* If there are only two possible outcomes that can occur in a given situation, then their probabilities must add up to 1.
>
> *Rule Two:* The probability of one *or* the other of two mutually exclusive outcomes occurring is the sum of their individual probabilities.
>
> *Rule Three:* When two events are *not* mutually exclusive, then the probability of the two events occurring together is *subtracted* from the sum of their individual probabilities.
>
> *Rule Four:* If two events are *independent,* the probability that they *both* could happen is found by multiplying their individual probabilities.
>
> *Rule Five:* If two events are *dependent,* the probability that they *both* could happen is found by multiplying the probability for the first event occurring by the probability of the second event occurring, when it is certain that the first event has occurred.

Examples   ■ *Rule One:* There are only two possibilities with regard to the gender of a newborn baby: It will be either a boy or a girl. The probability of having a boy is .51; the probability of having a girl is .49. Thus, .51 + .49 = 1.00 (see Figure 9.9).

■ *Rule Two:*

   • The probability that *either* Mr. Brown *or* Mrs. Brown will win the lottery is the sum of their separate probabilities (i.e., about .0000001 + .0000001 = .0000002).

   • The probability of drawing *either* the King of Hearts *or* the Queen of Spades in one draw from an honest deck of cards is $\frac{1}{52} + \frac{1}{52}$ or .038 (see Figure 9.10).

■ *Rule Three:* An employer wishes to diversify the company's workforce by employing more women and people of color. The applicant pool indicates that 40% are women and 30% are persons of color and that 15% of the women are women of color.

The probability of selecting a woman from the applicant pool is .4. The probability of getting a person of color is .3. But we cannot just add the two probabilities as we did with Rule Two, because an applicant could be *both* a woman and a person of color. Hence, the probability of obtaining a woman of color, using Rule Three, is .40 + .30 − .15, or .55. Subtracting .15 is the correction necessary to avoid double counting the possibility of selecting a woman of color.

- *Rule Four:*
  - The probability that *both* Mr. Brown *and* Mrs. Brown will win the lottery is the product of their separate probabilities (i.e., about .0000001 × .0000001, or—you get the idea!)
  - A telephone survey company needs to reach six identified businesses. If the probability of having an operator reach each on the first call is 1/2, or .50, what is the probability of contacting all six on the first call? It is

$$\frac{1}{2} \times \frac{1}{2} \times \frac{1}{2} \times \frac{1}{2} \times \frac{1}{2} \times \frac{1}{2}, \text{ or } \frac{1}{64} \ (.016).$$

- *Rule Five:*
  - What is the probability of randomly drawing two jacks successively from a well-shuffled, complete deck of playing cards without replacement? This is the same as asking: What is the probability of obtaining a jack on the second draw, *given* that one jack has already been drawn? In applying Rule Five in this case, we first determine the probability of getting a jack on the first draw. Since there are four jacks, and a total of 52 cards, the probability is 4/52, or .077. We next determine the probability of getting a jack on the second draw. Since the first jack has already been drawn, only three remain, and the number of cards still in the deck has been reduced by one to 51. Hence the probability of obtaining a jack on the second draw is 3/51, or .059. To apply Rule Five, therefore, we multiply the two: .077 times .059, which equals .0045; this is the probability of drawing two jacks in a row.
  - Suppose a sample of 50 people is to be selected randomly *without replacement* from a population with 140 members in which 74 are Caucasian, 31 Hispanic, 23 African American, and 12 Asian. What is the probability that both the first and second individuals selected will be Asian? The two selection

events are dependent because the probability for the second selection is affected by the fact that a previous selection was made that reduced both the number of Asians remaining and the size of the total group from which the second selection is to be made. The probability that the first individual selected would be Asian is 12/140. The probability that the second person would also be Asian is 11/139 (because there are only 11 Asians remaining and only 139 left in the total group). The probability, therefore, that both the first and second persons selected will be Asian, according to Rule Five, is 12/140 × 11/139, or .086 × .079 = .0068.

See also Conditional probability; independence; mutually exclusive outcomes; probability.

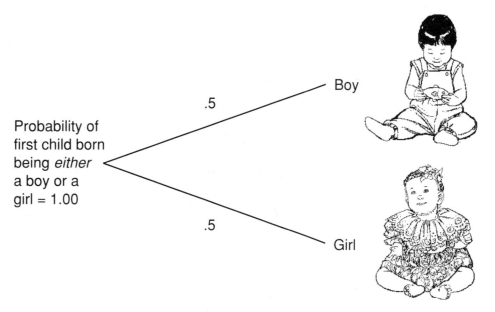

FIGURE 9.9 THE PROBABILITY OF ONLY TWO POSSIBLE OUT-COMES ALWAYS EQUALS 1.00.

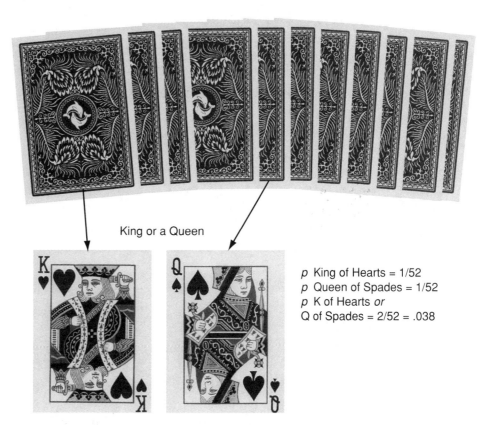

King or a Queen

p King of Hearts = 1/52
p Queen of Spades = 1/52
p K of Hearts *or*
Q of Spades = 2/52 = .038

FIGURE 9.10 THE PROBABILITY OF DRAWING *EITHER* THE KING OF HEARTS *OR* THE QUEEN OF SPADES IN ONE DRAW FROM AN HONEST DECK OF 52 PLAYING CARDS

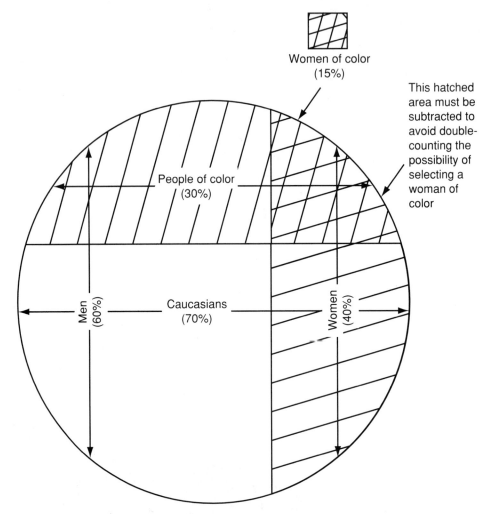

FIGURE 9.11 THE LIKELIHOOD OF SELECTING A WOMAN OF COLOR

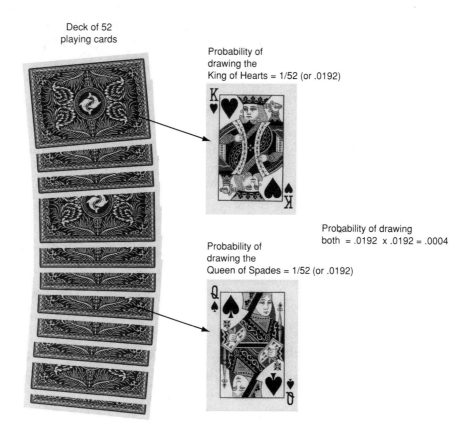

FIGURE 9.12 THE PROBABILITY OF DRAWING *BOTH* THE KING OF HEARTS AND THE QUEEN OF SPADES IN TWO DRAWS FROM AN HONEST DECK OF 52 PLAYING CARDS

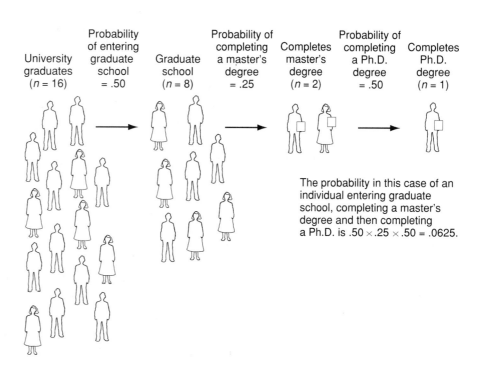

FIGURE 9.13 THE PROBABILITY OF AN INDIVIDUAL COMPLETING A PH.D. DEGREE

Binomial Distribution

Description The **binomial distribution** tells us how many times we can expect to get a predicted outcome or result when only two outcomes or results are possible, such as pass/fail; yes/no; or heads/tails.

A binomial distribution occurs when the following conditions exist:

- A series of events occur in which each particular occurrence is one trial.
- Each trial results in one of two outcomes.
- The outcomes from trial to trial are independent. That is, the probability of an outcome for any particular trial is not influenced by the outcome of any other trial.
- The probability of a particular outcome occurring is the same from trial to trial.

Examples
- The risk of transmitting the human immunodeficiency virus (HIV) continues to be a major health concern in the United States and elsewhere. Suppose a physician who works in a university health clinic, worried that the risk is increasing among the student body, surveys a sample of 600 students who visit the health clinic about their sexual behavior. She finds that 422 of these students are sexually active. One of the questions she asks is whether the students would be willing to lie to their partner about having a negative HIV-antibody test. Since their answer to this question is either "yes" or "no," the binomial distribution can be applied. There are, in effect, 422 "trials" of the experiment (i.e., how the students answer the question). Note that we assume that each trial has the same probability of lying or not.

- Suppose you toss an ordinary penny four times and record the results. What is the probability of getting a head all four times you toss the coin? The probability distribution is shown in Table 9.1. You can see that the probability of getting a head in all four tosses is very small (.0625). The probability of tossing only one head is .2500. To calculate the probability of getting two *or* more heads, add together the probabilities of getting exactly two, three, and four heads = .6875.

See also Categorical variable; independence; probability.

TABLE 9.1 Probability Distribution of Getting Different Numbers of Heads in Four Tosses

Number of Heads	Probability
0	.0625
1	.2500
2	.3750
3	.2500
4	.0625

Odds

Description   The **odds** of something is the ratio of an event occurring to its not occurring. Odds represent one of the two basic ways (the other is probability) that exist to indicate the chances that a randomly selected individual or event will fall into a particular category. If the probability that an event will occur is p, the odds that it will occur are p to $(1 - p)$.

Examples
- The odds of drawing, at random, a spade from a well-shuffled and unused deck of 52 playing cards are 13 to 39, or 1 *to* 3. By way of contrast, the *probability* (i.e., the likelihood) of drawing a spade is 1 *out* of 4, or .25.

- Suppose that 60% of the students at a large urban university have applied for financial aid. The odds that a student has applied for financial aid at this university, therefore, would be 6 to 4 (or 3 to 2, or 1.5 to 1).

- The odds *against* a high school basketball player playing professional basketball are estimated to be greater than 1000 to 1.

- The odds against throwing a "6" with a single die (in one throw) are 5 to 1.

- Thirty-seven of the 92 patients in a nursing home are men, and the remaining 55 are women. The probability of randomly selecting a man from the total group of patients is, therefore 37/92, or approximately .40. The odds of selecting a man would be .40 to $(1 - .40)$, or .40 to .60, or 2 to 3.

See also   Odds ratio; probability.

FIGURE 9.14   WHAT ARE THE ODDS?

Odds Ratio

Description   The **odds ratio** is the ratio of the odds of one categorical variable occurring to the odds of another. The **odds ratio** is a measure of association, but in this case, 1.00 means that there is no relationship between the two variables. The size of any relationship that does exist is measured by the difference (in either direction) from 1.00. An odds ratio greater than 1.00 indicates a positive relationship; an odds ratio of less than 1.00 indicates a negative relationship.

To compute the odds ratio for two categorical variables, you first calculate the odds of each variable occurring and then take the ratio of those odds.

Example   In 1993, researchers reported data on more than 6000 women who participated in the first National Health and Nutrition Examination Study.[1] The independent variable was whether a woman gave birth to her first child when she was 25 years of age or older. The dependent variable was whether she did or did not develop breast cancer. These data are shown in Table 9.2.

Let us calculate the odds of developing breast cancer for women having their first child at age 25 or older. It is 31 to 1,597, or .0194. The odds of developing breast cancer for women having their first child before age 25 is 65 to 4475, or .0145. The odds ratio, then, would be .0194/.0145 = 1.34. The odds of developing breast cancer, therefore, is 1.34 times greater for women who have their first child when they are 25 or older than if they have their first birth before age 25. Note that we know this only for the sample, however. It may not be true for the population. (This could be evaluated by calculating the chi-square statistic.)

See also   Odds; probability.

---

[1]M. Pagano and K. Gaureau, 1993. *Principles of biostatistics:* Belmont, CA, Duxbury Press.

TABLE 9.2 Relationship between Age of Mother When First Child Was Born and the Development of Breast Cancer

First Child at Age 25 or Older	Developed Breast Cancer	Did Not Develop Breast Cancer	Total
Yes	31	1597	1628
No	65	4475	4540
Total	96	6072	6168

Set 10

The concepts in this section are concerned with making decisions about populations based on information obtained on a sample. Provided that certain assumptions are met, it is legitimate to generalize from a sample to a population and, at the same time, determine the extent of error or inaccuracy in doing so.

Inferential Reasoning

Point versus Interval Estimate

Description   A **point estimate** is an estimate of a population parameter based on a statistic obtained from a sample. An interval estimate predicts that the population parameter is between two specified values.

Example   Suppose an office manager in a large manufacturing firm surveys a sample of the workers in the headquarters office to get their opinion about an office policy on working overtime. Imagine that, on a scale of 1 to 10, the average (mean) rating that the sample of office workers gives the new policy is 4.7. The manager can then conclude that 4.7 would be the best estimate of the average rating that the entire population of office workers would give the policy; that is, 4.7 is the manager's best estimate of what the average rating would have been if all of the office workers in the firm had been surveyed. The manager's estimate in this case is a *point* estimate. On the other hand, if the manager estimated that the average rating that the population would give would be somewhere *between* 4.2 and 5.2, he or she would be making an *interval* estimate.

See also   Bias; confidence interval; mean; normal distribution; standard deviation.

FIGURE 10.1 POINT VERSUS INTERVAL ESTIMATES

Confidence Interval

Description A **confidence interval** is the range within which a population value is predicted to lie on the basis of a sample value—and with a known probability of error. Its use requires that specific conditions be met, the most important being that the sample has been randomly selected.

Examples
- If the average annual income of a random sample of stockbrokers is $150,000, we may be able to say that the average annual income for *all* stockbrokers is between $75,000 and $225,000, with a 1 in 100 probability of being wrong.
- If a poll shows that 61% of people in a sample think that the President of the United States is doing a good job, we may be able to say that the entire population would give an approval rating between 56 and 66%, with a probability of only 1 in 1,000 of being wrong.

See also Normal distribution; population/sample; probability; sampling distribution.

FIGURE 10.2 WE CAN BE 99% CONFIDENT.

Standard Error

Description The **standard error** is an index of the stability of a particular statistic (such as the mean) that has been obtained for a particular sample. The smaller the standard error, the better the sample statistic (e.g., a sample mean) is as an estimate of the population parameter (i.e., the population mean). The standard error is a measure of *sampling error;* it refers to errors in our estimates due to random fluctuations in the samples we select. The standard error is the standard deviation of the sampling distribution of a statistic.

For example, the standard error of the mean indicates how much the mean of a single sample is likely to differ from the mean of a population. The smaller the standard error, the better the mean of the sample is as an estimate of the mean of the population. In short, the standard error answers the question: "How good an estimate of the population parameter (e.g., the population mean) is the sample statistic (e.g., the sample mean)?"

Examples ■ The mean diameter of a random sample of 200 redwood trees in a state park is found to be 28 inches, with a standard deviation of 12 inches. The standard error of the mean is calculated to be .85. Since a sampling distribution of means is a normal distribution, 95% of the time the sample mean will be (approximately) between ±2 standard deviations (i.e., standard errors) from the mean, or between 26.3 and 29.7 inches [28 ± 2(.85) inches].

■ Inspectors find that out of a random sample of 150 windshields taken from a production line, nine (6%) shatter under expected stress conditions. In this example, the standard error is found to be 2.9%. Since the sampling distribution is a normal distribution, the percent defective would be between 0.2% and 11.8% in 95% of a large number of samples inspected [6% ± 2 (2.9%)].

See also Mean; standard deviation.

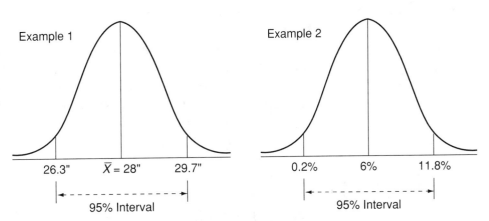

FIGURE 10.3 STANDARD ERRORS

Research Hypothesis

Description
A **research hypothesis** (also known as an *alternative hypothesis*) states that there *is* a change, a relationship, or an effect. It is likely to be the hypothesis that the researcher believes is true. The procedure is to first test the *null* hypothesis. If the null hypothesis can be rejected, the research hypothesis is supported—though not proven. If the null hypothesis is *not* rejected, the research hypothesis is rejected.

Example
An executive believes that soundproofing walls and ceilings in offices will result in higher productivity and morale. She persuades her board of directors to install soundproofing in three offices. Her research hypothesis is that the effect of the soundproofing will be higher output, on the average, than for employees in offices that are not soundproofed. However, the null hypothesis that will actually be tested is that there is no difference (other than what is due to chance) in the average scores for the two groups. The alternative hypothesis should be retained *only* if the null hypothesis *is* rejected.

See also
Null hypothesis.

FIGURE 10.4 RESEARCH HYPOTHESES

Null Hypothesis

Description   A **null hypothesis** is the hypothesis that is actually tested in using a procedure for checking on statistical significance. It most often is a statement that there is no change, no relationship, no difference, or no effect. In other words, it often says that any change or difference that is found in analysis of the data can be attributed to chance sampling errors. An alternative hypothesis (also known as the *research hypothesis*) states that there *is* a change, a relationship, or an effect. It is likely to be the hypothesis that the researcher believes. The procedure is to first test the null hypothesis. If the null hypothesis can be rejected, the research hypothesis may be correct. If the null hypothesis is *not* rejected, the research hypothesis is rejected.

Example   An elementary school principal believes that playing classical music in classrooms will result in students learning more and thereby scoring higher on a standardized achievement test. She persuades the school officials to install CD players in three classrooms. Her research hypothesis is that the effect of playing classical music will be higher scores, on the average, than for students in classrooms where classical music is not played. However, the null hypothesis that will actually be tested is that there is no difference (other than what is due to chance) in the average scores for the two groups. The research hypothesis should be retained *only* if the null hypothesis *is* rejected.

See also   Research hypothesis; statistical significance.

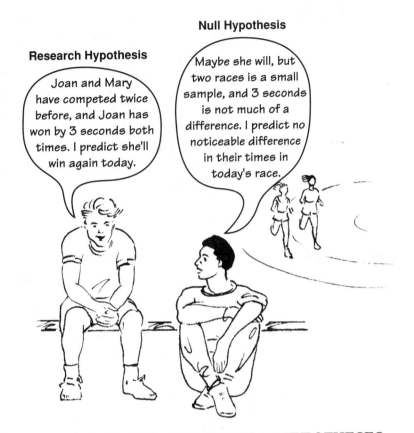

FIGURE 10.5   TWO KINDS OF HYPOTHESES

Statistical Significance

Description An outcome is **statistically significant** when it is highly unlikely to have occurred by chance or, more precisely, as a result of *sampling error*. Provided that the necessary assumptions are met, the probability of a chance outcome can be precisely determined. If the probability is sufficiently small, the outcome is statistically significant. It is customary to specify particular probabilities that will be considered significant; these are called significance levels or *alpha levels*. The most common are .05, .01, and .001. Statistical significance should not be confused with *practical (substantive) significance*.

Examples
- A difference between the means of men and women on a test of self-esteem is reported as statistically significant at the .01 level. This means that a difference in means as large as the one obtained would occur less than 1 time in 100 by chance. This statement is correct provided that all assumptions have been met—the most important being that both samples were randomly selected.

- A correlation coefficient of .38 was found to be statistically significant at the .01 level. This means that the chance that the true population correlation coefficient was 0.00 (and that the .38 value was due merely to sampling fluctuations) was no more than 1 in 100.

See also Normal distribution; null hypothesis; probability; sampling error.

FIGURE 10.6   IS IT STATISTICALLY SIGNIFIANCE?

Type I Error

Description A **type I error** occurs when the null hypothesis is rejected when it is in fact true. If the right conditions exist, the likelihood of making this error can be determined.

Examples
- Imagine that a market researcher hypothesizes that most people prefer Pepsi over Coke. The null hypothesis would be that there is no difference in people's preferences between Pepsi and Coke. To test the hypothesis, the researcher chooses a sample of people to take a taste test, wherein they are asked to taste both soft drinks (in unmarked paper cups, same amount, same temperature, etc.).

  A type I error here (rejecting the null hypothesis when you really shouldn't) would be concluding that the sample indicates that people like Pepsi when most people really show no preference between the two soft drinks. By way of contrast, a type II error (not rejecting the null hypothesis when you really should) would be concluding that there is no difference in preference when most people actually prefer Pepsi.

- Consider another example. Caitlin Johnson's parents, worried about some symptoms she is displaying, hypothesize that she has pneumonia (a research hypothesis). The null hypothesis is that she does not have pneumonia.

  They take her to a pediatrician, who tells them that Caitlin's lungs are congested. He says that congestion like that in Caitlin's lungs tends to occur only 5 times out of 100 (5% of the time) in children who do *not* have pneumonia. He therefore recommends treatment. He admits that there is a 5% chance of a type I error in making such a recommendation—that is, that Caitlin actually does not have pneumonia and hence treatment is unnecessary.

See also Critical region; null hypothesis; probability; statistical significance; type II error.

FIGURE 10.7 A POSSIBLE TYPE I ERROR

Critical Region

Description The **critical region** contains those sample values that are very unlikely to be obtained by chance. They are indicated by the area in a sampling distribution that is considered "critical" to a particular study. The size of this area is determined by the alpha level. This region is considered critical because, if a sample statistic (e.g., a sample mean) falls in this region, the null hypothesis can be rejected.

Example Imagine that a researcher compares a standard medicine with an herbal medicine with respect to reducing asthma attacks. Over a six-month period, two treatment groups average 4.3 and 3.1 attacks. The null hypothesis is that the real difference (in the population) is zero. The researcher sets the *alpha level* at .01. She can then determine whether or not the difference in means (4.3 – 3.1 = 1.2) falls within her critical region. If so, she will reject the null hypothesis and conclude that one treatment is better than the other.

See also Analysis of covariance; analysis of variance; chi-square test; normal distribution; probability; statistical significance; *t*-test.

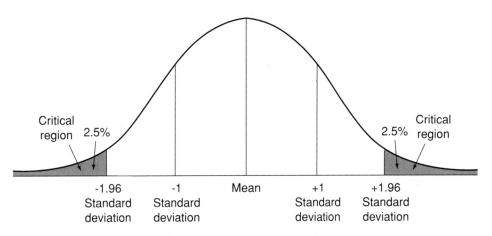

FIGURE 10.8 CRITICAL REGIONS

Alpha Level

Description   The **alpha level,** symbolized by α, is the chance a researcher is willing to take of committing a *type I error*—that is, of rejecting the null hypothesis when it is actually true. For the whole population, the smaller the alpha level, the smaller the chance that the research result (i.e., the outcome) was due simply to chance. Thus, an alpha level of .01 is more difficult to obtain than a level of .05. Also called *level of statistical significance*.

Example   A researcher conducts a study in which she compares the effects of two exercise routines on weight loss. Routine A involves riding a stationary bicycle for 25 minutes a day; Routine B involves using a rowing machine each day for 25 minutes. A total of 100 individuals are randomly assigned to one of the two routines. After a six-month period, she finds that the individuals who used the bicycles lost an average of 20 pounds, while those who rowed lost an average of 17 pounds. This difference of 3 pounds was found to be statistically significant at an alpha level of .05, indicating that it would happen only 5 times out of 100 by chance.

See also   Critical ratio; *p* value; statistical significance; one- versus two-tailed test of statistical significance.

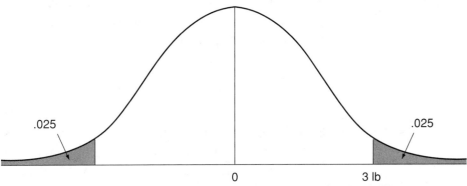

.025 .025

0

3 lb
Obtained difference
(bike riders lost an
average of 20 pounds;
rowers lost an
average of 17 pounds;
20 − 17 = 3 pounds)

Null hypothesis:
the difference in means
will equal 0

The probability of getting a difference as large
as 3 lbs. (an average weight loss of 3 lbs.) in favor
of *either* biking *or* rowing is .025 + .025 = .05,
which is the *alpha level*.

FIGURE 10.9   AN ALPHA LEVEL OF .05

Type II Error

Description   A **type II error** occurs if the null hypothesis is not rejected, when it is in fact false. If the right conditions exist, the likelihood of making this error can be determined. A type II error is typically represented as β (beta.)

Examples
- Josh Lennox's parents, worried over some symptoms (persistent coughing and a sore throat) that Josh is displaying, hypothesize that he has strep throat, a research hypothesis (the null hypothesis is that his symptoms are not due to strep throat). They take him to a pediatrician, who states that congestion like that found in Josh's lungs occurs about 1% of the time in children who do *not* have strep throat. She concludes that Josh does not have strep throat. (Maybe he has a cold.) She recommends against treatment.

  But if Josh really *does* have strep throat, the physician is wrong, and her decision not to pursue treatment for Josh could have tragic consequences. She will have made a type II error.

- A pharmaceutical researcher believes that one cough medicine commonly sold over the counter in many drugstores is more effective than another. She obtains a sample of individuals who have been using each cough medicine, and asks them if it was effective. She then divides the number reporting who say "yes" by the total number of individuals in each sample to obtain a proportion. She decides that she will reject the null hypothesis only if the results were significant at the .01 level. She conducts a test for the statistical significance of the difference in proportions, and finds that it is significant at the .04 level. She does not, therefore, reject the null hypothesis. Many researchers believe that a p value of .05 or smaller justifies rejection of the null hypothesis. It is possible, therefore, that she has committed a type II error.

See also   Critical region; null hypothesis; p value; probability; statistical significance; type I error.

FIGURE 10.10 A POSSIBLE TYPE II ERROR

Power of a Statistical Test

Description   The **power of a statistical test** is the probability that the null hypothesis *will* be rejected when it is correct to do so because it is, in fact, false. It is expressed as 1-β, where β is the probability of not rejecting the null hypothesis when it is false (a Type II error). When the null hypothesis refers to differences between averages, power is the probability that a true difference in *population* averages will be concluded to exist on the basis of an obtained *sample* difference. Some statistical tests are more powerful than others as applied to a particular set of data. Parametric tests (e.g., ANOVA) are generally more powerful than nonparametric tests (e.g., Chisquare). Power curves are a method of comparing the power of different statistical tests that might be applied to the same data. The power of the test is plotted against a series of possible "true" values such as differences in means.

The power of a statistical test is in some ways like the power of a telescope. Astronomers looking at the planets Mars and Venus with a low-power telescope probably can see that they look like spheres, but it is unlikely that they can see much by way of differences in terrain—such as mountains, valleys, and canyons. With an extremely high-power telescope, however, they can see such differences. When the purpose of a statistical test is to check on differences, power is the likelihood that the test will correctly yield a conclusion that there *are* differences when, in fact, differences actually exist.

Example   Suppose a basketball coach wants to study the effectiveness of a new coaching technique for shooting free throws. She selects a sample of high school girls and asks each to shoot 30 free throws. They are given the same "test" again after she coaches them using her new technique. The mean number of baskets before coaching is 14.3, but it is 20.7 after coaching—a difference of 6.4. The coach's null hypothesis is that any positive difference (i.e., the number of baskets before coaching subtracted from the number of baskets after coaching) is due to a chance departure from the true population difference of zero (using a one-tailed test of statistical significance). A *t*-test is used to test for statistical significance.

See also   Critical region; normal distribution; null hypothesis; probability; statistical significance; test statistic.

In the preceding example, the critical value for rejecting the null hypothesis at the .05 level is calculated. Assume that it is 5.1. Any difference in means that is larger than +5.1 would result in rejecting the null hypothesis. Figure A in the two figures below illustrates these conditions:

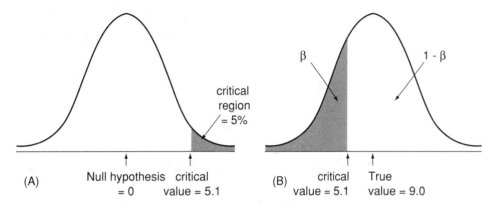

Next, assume that we somehow know that the "true" difference in the population is actually 9.0. This is shown in Figure B above. The shaded part of the figure shows the probability that we will not reject the null hypothesis (which we now know to be wrong) by using the critical value of 5.1, which is determined from a t-table. (See the Appendix.) This is β. The power under this particular "known" value of the population difference is $1-\beta$.

Next, the power ($1-\beta$) for a series of assumed "true" values can be obtained in the same way. When power is plotted against assumed values, the result looks something like what is shown in Figure C:

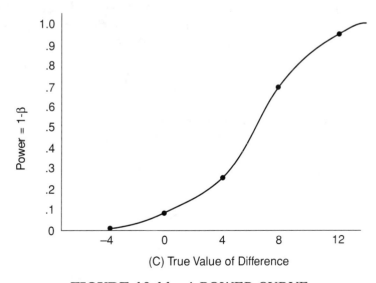

FIGURE 10.11   A POWER CURVE

One- versus Two-Tailed Tests of Statistical Significance

Description An investigator has a choice as to how to state the null hypothesis. If it is stated as "the obtained value is a chance variation from a predetermined population value," the presumption is that a sufficient deviation in *either* direction from the population value should lead to rejection of the null hypothesis. In this case, a two-tailed test is appropriate. Often, however, it is only a deviation in *one* direction that is of interest, in which case a one-tailed test can be used.

Examples
- A researcher compares two medical treatments without specifying ahead of time which one he predicts is better. A two-tailed test means that a sufficient difference in *either* direction (i.e., favoring *either* treatment) will lead to rejection of the null hypothesis. The difference between the means can fall in either tail of the distribution. Both tails are included in the alpha level. If alpha is .05, .025 is in each tail. The critical region includes *both* tails.
- A researcher compares a new medical treatment with an existing one. She is interested only in finding out whether the new treatment is better than the existing one. Should the new treatment be worse, the study is over. Since the researcher is predicting the direction of difference *ahead of time,* she is entitled to use a one-tailed test which places all of alpha (e.g., .05) in one tail. The critical region, in this case, lies in only *one* tail (see Figure 10.13).

See also Alpha level; critical region; normal distribution; null hypothesis; practical significance; research hypothesis; statistical significance; *t*-test.

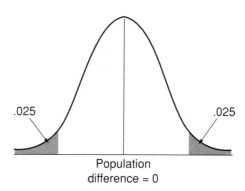

FIGURE 10.12 A TWO-TAILED TEST WITH α = .05

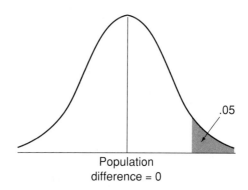

FIGURE 10.13 A ONE-TAILED TEST WITH α = .05

Parametric/Nonparametric Test

Description **Parametric tests** are called parametric because of certain assumptions about population parameters, which are basic to their mathematical derivation. The most important of these are (1) that the variable in question is distributed normally in the population and (2) that the variance is the same for each of two or more populations (or treatment groups) being compared. Under some circumstances, these assumptions have been shown to be *not* crucial to meaningful interpretation. This is known as the *robustness* of the statistic. The most commonly used parametric statistics are analysis of variance (ANOVA), analysis of covariance (ANCOVA), multivariate analysis of variance (MANOVA), and the *t*-test. Parametric tests also assume an *interval scale*, which is often not known to be the case.

When the assumptions of parametric tests are seriously violated, **nonparametric tests** should be considered. Nonparametric tests make no assumption about population parameters, nor do they assume an interval scale, since data are treated as categorical or ordinal. Their disadvantage is that they are generally less powerful, and hence their use is more likely to cause the null hypothesis not to be rejected when it should be. The most commonly used nonparametrics are chi-square, the Mann-Whitney *U* test, the sign test, and the Wilcoxon signed ranks test for matched samples.

Examples ■ In comparing two antidepressant medications, a researcher finds one to be, on the average, more effective than the other. The difference is determined by a *t*-test to be statistically significant. However, he discovers that his two samples have larger than chance disparities in variance and in departure from a normal distribution. These raise questions about the appropriateness of the *t*-test, so a *nonparametric test* could be used instead of the (parametric) *t*-test.

■ An economist compares a sample of companies in which workers are major shareholders with a sample of companies in which they are not. The variable studied is employee satisfaction. A nonparametric test indicates that the difference in means is not statistically significant. She decides to use a parametric test, reasoning that it is more likely to show significance and that the assumptions required seem likely to be met. If they are not, she faces a dilemma.

See also Experiment; nonparametric test; one- versus two-tailed test of statistical significance; ordinal scale; power of a statistical test; statistical significance.

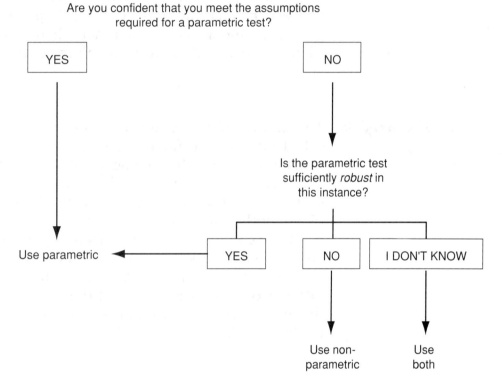

Are you confident that you meet the assumptions required for a parametric test?

| YES | NO |

Is the parametric test sufficiently *robust* in this instance?

Use parametric ← | YES | | NO | | I DON'T KNOW |

Use non-parametric

Use both

FIGURE 10.14 SHOULD YOU USE A PARAMETRIC OR NONPARAMETRIC TEST?

t-Test

Description The *t*-test is a test to determine whether the difference between two group means is statistically significant. *t*-tests are also used to determine whether correlation coefficients and regression coefficients are statistically significant. The value required for significance depends on the sample size. When applied to differences between means, there are two versions. One is used when the groups are independent; the other when scores are correlated, as when pretests and posttests are given to the same individuals.

Example A researcher for a soft drink firm is planning to introduce a new soft drink targeted for teenagers. He picks a random sample of teens, gives them their favorite soft drink in an unmarked can, and then asks each individual in the group to rate the drink on a scale from 1 (very poor) to 50 (outstanding). The researcher then picks another random sample, gives each person in this group the drink the company plans to introduce (also in an unmarked can), and asks each person to rate it on the same scale. The researcher determines whether the mean rating of their favorite soft drink differs from the mean rating of the new drink and, if the ratings do differ, uses a *t*-test to find out whether this difference is statistically significant.

See also Mean; probability; statistical significance.

FIGURE 10.15 *t*-TESTS

Analysis of Variance (ANOVA)

Description   **Analysis of variance (ANOVA)** is a procedure for determining whether obtained differences between the means of two *or more* groups are due to chance. ANOVA is actually a more general test than the *t*-test that is appropriate to use with three or more groups (it can also be used with two groups). Variation both within and between groups is analyzed statistically, yielding what is known as an *F* value. This *F* value is then checked in a statistical table (see the Appendix) to see whether it is statistically significant (i.e., not due to chance). The larger the obtained value of *F*, the greater the likelihood that statistical significance exists. When more than two groups are compared, the *F*-test will not by itself indicate which pair of means (if any) are significantly different. A further (quite simple) procedure called a post hoc analysis is required to find this out. ANOVA is also used when more than one independent variable is investigated. This procedure requires a number of assumptions, the most important of which is that the groups are randomly selected from the populations they represent.

Example   The floor supervisor of a small plant that manufactures shoes wishes to check the quality of output on three of the plant's assembly lines. Random samples of pairs of shoes from each line are selected over several days, and the number of unacceptable pairs are identified for each day. The average number of unacceptable pairs for each assembly line is then calculated. An analysis of variance test indicates a difference in the number of unacceptable pairs among the three production lines that is unlikely to have occurred by chance. Further analysis (see *pairwise comparison*) is needed to determine which of the difference(s) are greater than chance. Figure 10.16 suggests that it is likely that the difference between assembly lines 1 and 2 is greater than chance, whereas the difference between 1 and 3 may or may not be.

See also   Factorial design; mean; probability; statistical significance; variance.

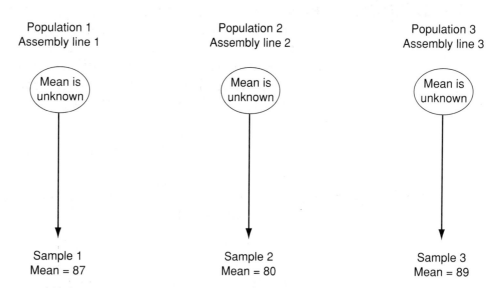

FIGURE 10.16 TYPICAL SITUATION IN WHICH ANOVA WOULD BE USED

Between-Group Differences

Description **Between-group differences** are the differences between the groups being studied, typically in an *analysis of variance;* usually contrasted with the differences that exist *within* these groups. The differences between the means of two or more groups are considered large (and thus statistically significant) only if they are large when compared with the differences among scores within the groups.

Example Suppose we conduct an experiment in which we obtain the results shown in Table 10.1.

TABLE 10.1 Between-Group Differences

	Experimental Group	Control Group
	40	65
	38	64
	35	59
	32	58
	30	54
Total	175	300
Mean	35	60

The between-groups difference appears to be a real difference (i.e., unlikely to be due to chance) because it is large in comparison with the differences within each of the groups (one would use ANOVA here to test for statistical significance).

Figure 10.17 shows that the difference in means (25 points) is large compared to the differences within each group.

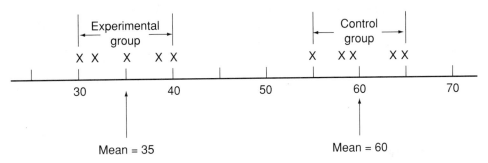

FIGURE 10.17 BETWEEN-GROUP DIFFERENCES

Interaction Effect

Description An **interaction effect** results from combining particular combinations of variables. It is different from, or in addition to, what would be expected if effects were simply cumulative. Analysis of variance procedures enable the testing of the statistical significance of such an effect with quantitative data.

Examples
- The combination of hydrogen and oxygen in 2 to 1 molecular proportions (H_2O) produces a substance—water—that would not be expected if we consider the properties of hydrogen and oxygen separately.
- Student characteristics may combine with teaching method to provide a different outcome than would be expected from a straightforward consideration of their separate effects. Suppose the results of a study of method and student characteristics show that the discussion method results in higher self-esteem scores than the lecture method and that the extrovert characteristic results in higher scores than the introvert. This is shown in the graphs in Figure 10.18. However, in the right-hand graph (but not in the left-hand one), there is an additional effect resulting from the combination of characteristic and method; that is, the combination of discussion method and extrovert characteristic results in an additional increment to the mean score. In the left-hand graph, extroverts score higher than introverts under both lecture and discussion methods. In the right-hand graph, however, the difference between extroverts and introverts is considerably greater under the discussion method, indicating an interaction between method of teaching and student characteristic.

See also ANOVA (analysis of variance).

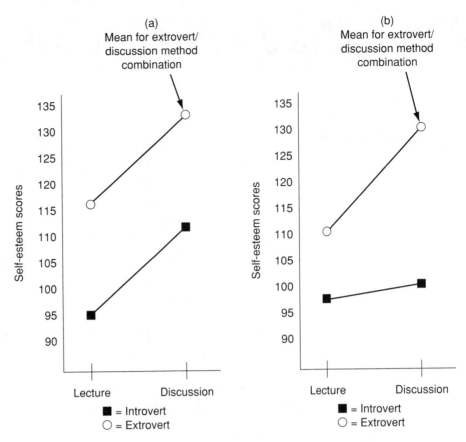

FIGURE 10.18 INTERACTION BETWEEN STUDENT
CHARACTERISTICS AND TEACHING METHOD

Moderate drinking can be fun. . . as can a drive in the country. . .

but not the interaction.

FIGURE 10.19 AN INTERACTION EFFECT

Pairwise Comparison

Description   **Pairwise comparison** involves going back through the data in an analysis of variance, after the analysis has been completed to compare the means for different treatment groups two at a time. Analysis of variance alone enables one to determine *only* whether *one or more* of the differences among means are statistically significant, *not* which differences between particular pairs of means are large enough to be statistically significant. Pairwise comparison is needed, therefore, when there are three or more treatments, to determine which particular pairs of group means are statistically significant and which are not. The statistical methods for making pairwise comparisons are called *post hoc tests*. There are two categories of post hoc tests: *a priori tests* (also called planned comparisons) for making comparisons of treatment groups that are decided on before the start of the experiment, and *a posteriori tests*, for making comparisons that may not have been planned at the beginning of the study. A posteriori tests are used only when the overall analysis of variance test is statistically significant.

Example   A research project was conducted to determine the relationship of type of occupation to a measure of stress. Ten men in each of three categories of occupation were studied: groups A, B, and C. Their scores on the stress measure are shown in Table 10.2. The mean for group A was 77.1, for group B, 66.8, and for group C, 74.2. Analysis of variance showed that at least one of the differences between these pairs of means was statistically significant. A posteriori tests were run to find out which particular pairs of means differed significantly. The means for groups A and B did differ significantly, but the difference between means for group A compared to group C was not significant, nor was the difference for groups B and C.

See also   Analysis of variance (ANOVA); mean; statistical significance; variance.

TABLE 10.2 Relationship of Type of Occupation to Level of Stress

Group A		Group B		Group C	
69	82	66	71	51	71
85	81	55	70	83	82
78	66	72	75	72	79
87	70	66	68	86	71
82	71	59	66	74	73
Mean = 77.1		Mean = 66.8		Mean = 74.2	

Difference between the means of group A and group B *is* statistically significant (77.1 − 66.8 = 10.3). But difference between B and C is not: (74.2 − 66.8 = 7.4) and difference between A and C also is not: (77.1 − 74.2 = 2.9).

Multivariate Analysis of Variance (MANOVA)

Description **Multivariate analysis of variance (MANOVA)** differs from analysis of variance in only one respect: It incorporates two or more dependent variables in the same analysis, allowing a more complete test of possible differences among means. MANOVA allows for the simultaneous study of two or more *related* dependent variables while controlling for any correlations among them. If the dependent variables are not related in some way, it makes no sense to do a MANOVA; instead, a separate ANOVA for each of the unrelated dependent variables should be performed.

Example Suppose a researcher wishes to study the effects of a daily bike ride over hilly terrain on the heart rate of a group of 50-year-old males. The researcher could use ANOVA to test the (null) hypothesis that there is no difference in the average (mean) heart rate of three groups: men who ride one mile a day, men who ride two miles a day, and men who don't ride at all. The use of MANOVA makes it possible to add other (related) dependent variables to the design, such as average blood pressure, weight, and respiratory rate and determine whether the groups differ on a composite of all four variables.

See also Analysis of variance (ANOVA); dependent/independent variables; statistical significance.

FIGURE 10.20   MANOVA

Analysis of Covariance (ANCOVA)

Description

Analysis of covariance (ANCOVA) is a variation of analysis of variance that is used when two or more groups are to be equated on a pretest or other variable that is related in some way to the dependent variable. Analysis of covariance enables one to mathematically adjust the posttest mean scores on the dependent variable for each group to compensate for initial differences between groups on the variables to be controlled. The variable or variables to be controlled are called *covariates*.

As in analysis of variance, ANCOVA produces an *F* value, which is then looked up in a statistical table (see the Appendix) to see if it is statistically significant. ANCOVA does require a number of assumptions, the most important being that the groups were randomly selected from the populations they represent.

ANCOVA is sometimes used in experimental studies to remove the effects of one or more other variables or in quasi-experimental studies when subjects cannot be randomly assigned to different groups. It is also used at times in nonexperimental studies, such as surveys of nonrandom samples, although this kind of usage is controversial.

Example

A statistically significant difference of 15 points is found between the average (mean) growth (in inches) of trees receiving two different nutrient treatments. It is suspected, however, that the two groups of trees may have differed initially on such variables as genetic stock, make-up of the soil in which they were planted, and the amount of water available. If each of these extraneous variables can be measured, they can be controlled mathematically by using ANCOVA. It can then be determined whether the difference of 15 points that was initially found is still statistically significant.

See also

Analysis of variance (ANOVA); dependent/independent variables; mean; statistical significance.

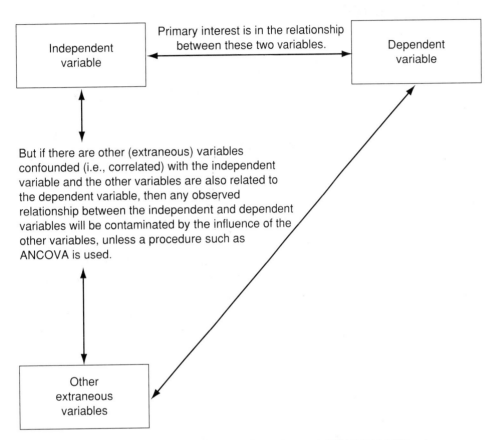

FIGURE 10.21 ANALYSIS OF COVARIANCE

Sign Test

Description   The **sign test** is a nonparametric statistical test that is used when a researcher wants to analyze two related (as opposed to independent) samples and is uncomfortable with the assumptions that are required for more powerful parametric tests. Related samples are connected in some way. For example, often a researcher will try to equalize groups on IQ, gender, age, or some other variable. The groups are *matched*, so to speak, on these variables. Another example of a related sample is when the same group is both pretested and posttested (that is, tested twice). In other words, each individual is tested on two different occasions (as with the *t*-test for correlated means).

The sign test is very easy to use. The researcher simply lines up the pairs of related subjects and then determines how many times the paired subjects in one group scored higher than those in the other group. If the groups do not differ significantly, the totals for the two groups should be about equal. If there is a marked difference in the number of times one group scores higher than the other, the difference may be statistically significant. The probability of this occurrence can be determined by consulting the appropriate statistical table.

Example   Two groups of 10 students each are matched according to IQ, and then each group uses a different textbook in their respective statistics class. At the end of the semester, the scores for each matched pair of students are compared. The students in Group B score higher in 8 of the 10 pairs, which is a noticeable difference in the totals for the two groups. It is very likely that a difference this large is statistically significant.

See also   Median; nonparametric test; statistical significance.

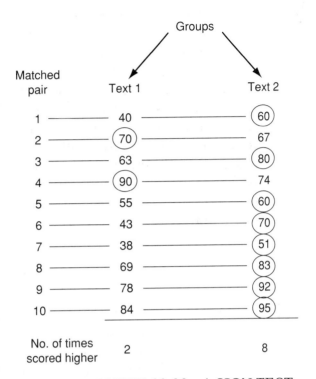

FIGURE 10.22 A SIGN TEST

Mann-Whitney *U* Test

Description   The **Mann-Whitney *U* test** is a nonparametric alternative to the *t*-test used when a researcher wishes to analyze ranked data. The scores from two groups that have been given different treatments are obtained, intermingled, and then ranked as if they were all from just one group. The logic of the test is as follows: If the two groups are essentially similar (i.e., if the treatments did not produce a noticeable difference), then the sum of the pooled rankings for *each* group should be about the same. If the summed ranks are markedly different, on the other hand, then this difference is likely to be statistically significant, indicating the difference was not due to chance. The test produces a value (*U*). The probability of occurrence can then be checked in the appropriate statistical table to see if its likelihood is more than chance.

Example   A psychologist develops a test of manual dexterity for three-year-olds. He randomly selects a sample of 10 boys and 10 girls, all three-year-olds, at a daycare center, and has each child arrange a set of seven blocks in order from largest to smallest. He then records how long it takes each child to arrange the blocks. Their times are as follows:

> Girls: 28, 25, 18, 21, 16, 26, 17, 43, 35, 36
> Boys: 13, 29, 15, 10, 8, 9, 12, 27, 7, 22

Let us designate the girls as sample G and the boys as sample B. When we combine the two samples and arrange the scores in rank order, we get the results shown in Table 10.3.

As you can see, the summed ranks for the two groups are quite different, suggesting it is quite likely that this difference is *not* due to chance.

See also   Nonparametric test; ordinal scale; statistical significance.

TABLE 10.3   Ranking the Scores of Boys and Girls

Rank	1	2	3	4	5	6	7	8	9	10	11	12	13	14	15	16	17	18	19	20
Score	7	8	9	10	12	13	15	16	17	18	21	22	25	26	27	28	29	35	36	43
Sample	B	B	B	B	B	B	B	G	G	G	B	G	G	B	G	B	G	G	G	G

Sum for boys = 1 + 2 + 3 + 4 + 5 + 6 + 7 + 12 + 15 + 17 = 72   Difference = 138 − 72 = 66

Sum for girls = 8 + 9 + 10 + 11 + 13 + 14 + 16 + 18 + 19 + 20 = 138

Study 1

Sample A = X
Sample B = ■

Notice that most of the scores from sample A are clustered at one end of the rank ordering...

Likely to be statistically significant

Study 2

Sample A = X
Sample B = ■

...whereas here they are dispersed throughout.

Not likely to be statistically significant

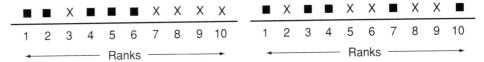

FIGURE 10.23   THE MANN-WHITNEY *U* TEST

Practical (Substantive) Significance

Description　**Practical significance,** or *substantive significance,* is a finding that reveals something of practical or real importance about that being studied. It is often used in contrast with *statistical significance,* which indicates that a result is unlikely to be due to chance alone.

Examples
- Suppose a large random sample of high school pitchers in New York City showed an average fastball speed of 75 mph, whereas a second sample in Los Angeles showed a mean fastball speed of 71 mph. This difference might be statistically significant because of the large sample size but few would say that it is of any practical importance.

- Suppose a new treatment for weight loss showed an average loss after six months of 20 pounds in a group of 15 overweight men, whereas a comparison group lost only 5 pounds. The 15-pound difference may well *not* be statistically significant (partly because of the small sample size), but it is of sufficient practical importance to warrant further study.

See also　Effect size; inferential statistics; statistical significance.

FIGURE 10.24 PRACTICAL SIGNIFICANCE

Effect Size

Description   **Effect size** is a numerical index indicating practical (substantive) significance—as distinct from statistical significance. There are a number of such indexes of which the most common is delta, or Δ. It is obtained by subtracting from the mean of a treatment group the mean of a meaningful comparison group—(ideally a control group receiving no treatment) and dividing by the standard deviation of the comparison group. It is particularly useful when there are no external standards of evaluation. It is not essential, for example, in comparing the average income of physicians with that of teachers, since the size of the difference is obviously considerable.

Examples
- In a particular pine forest, the mean tree diameter in 1883 was 16.6 inches; in 1994, it was 9.1 inches. How important is this difference of 7.5 inches? The standard deviation in 1994 was 10.1 inches. Delta equals 7.5/10.1 = .74. Using a commonly agreed upon (but ultimately arbitrary) standard of .50 for effect size, this difference would be considered of great practical significance.

- An economist finds that the difference in mean annual income between teachers in two industrial nations is $1000.00. He calculates that this is statistically significant at the .01 level. However, when he calculates an effect size (Δ), he obtains a value of .12, which suggests that the difference is of little practical significance (although some teachers might disagree).

- A large middle school in a depressed area of a city in the southeast had frequent problems of students getting into fights. The principal decided to introduce a special program in conflict resolution for all students. One month of existing records of the number of student fights of a random sample of students just before the program started were compared with the number for the next month. The average number of fights per student during the first month was 2.1, and 1.9 during the second month. The standard deviation during the second month was .86, so the effect size was (2.1 – 1.9) /.86, or .23, which is not even close to the standard of .50. The results of the program (at least so far), therefore, are not encouraging.

See also   Mean; standard deviation; *t*-test.

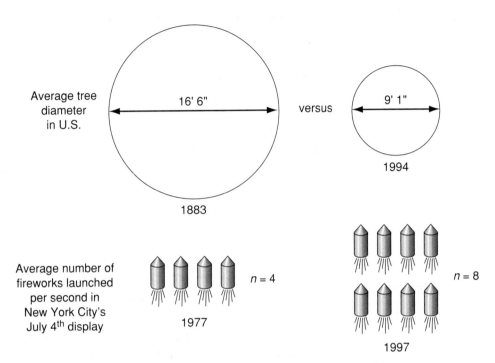

Average tree diameter in U.S.

16' 6" versus 9' 1"

1883 1994

Average number of fireworks launched per second in New York City's July 4th display

n = 4

1977

n = 8

1997

FIGURE 10.25 WHEN DOES A DIFFERENCE MAKE A DIFFERENCE?

Meta Analysis

Description   **Meta analysis** is a term applied to quantitative assessment of a number of studies (or data reports) on the same topic in an effort to reduce the subjectivity or judgment involved in the more traditional literature review. The most common index is effect size, which is determined for each study and then averaged or otherwise displayed. Although such analyses have become much more common in all fields, they are no panacea. Critics complain that the procedure fails to distinguish well-designed studies from poorly designed studies and makes no allowance for different sample sizes.

Example   One of the earliest meta analyses using effect size found an average effect size of .67 for 375 studies on the impact of psychotherapy. According to this, the average client was about two thirds of a standard deviation better off than a person receiving no treatment.[1] This finding provides support for claiming that the outcomes of psychotherapy are often of considerable practical importance.

See also   Analysis of variance (ANOVA); effect size; statistical significance; *t*-test.

---

[1]Smith, M.L, Glass, G.V, and Miller, T.J. (1980). *Benefits of Psychotherapy*. Baltimore, MD: Johns Hopkins University Press.

FIGURE 10.26 META ANALYSIS

Appendix Contents

A-1 How to Percentage a Table

To determine the percentage of cases (scores, etc.) that fall within each of the cells within a crossbreak table, the cases are divided into groups according to a certain characteristic. This is the *independent variable*. Each of these subgroups is then described in terms of another characteristic. This is the *dependent variable*. The number of cases falling in each cell can then be compared.

A sample of men and women are asked whether or not they favor sexual equality in the workplace. Gender is the independent variable. The individuals in the sample are then divided by gender into two groups—the men and women. Within each gender group, those who favor sexual equality are separated from those who do not favor it. Opinion about sexual equality is the dependent variable. Since there are two groups and two possible opinions (favor or not), there are four cells. Dividing the number in each cell by the total number in each group (e.g., the number of women in favor divided by the total number of women) and multiplying by 100 gives the percentage in each cell.

See also   Crossbreak table.

A. Some men and women who either favor sexual equality (yes) or do not favor it (no).

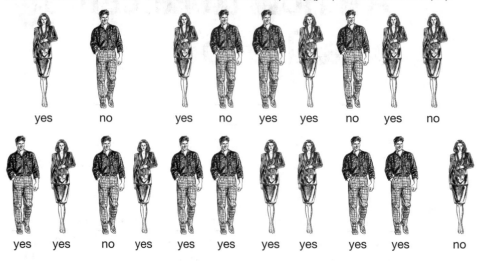

yes   no   yes   no   yes   yes   no   yes   no

yes   yes   no   yes   yes   yes   yes   yes   yes   yes   no

B. Separate the men and the women (the independent variable).

Women

Men

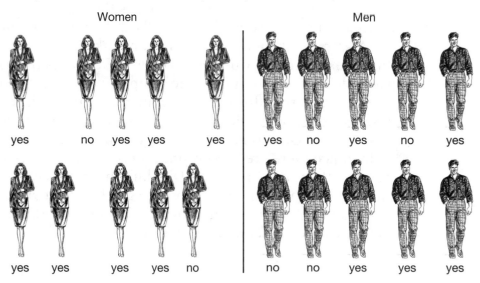

yes   no   yes   yes   yes   yes   no   yes   no   yes

yes   yes   yes   yes   no   no   no   yes   yes   yes

C. Within each gender group, separate those who favor equality from those who do not favor it.

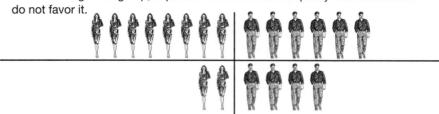

Count how many there are in each cell—8 women and 6 men in favor; 2 women and 4 men against. What percentage of the women favor equality? of the men?

	Women	Men
Favor equality	80%	60%
Don't favor equality	20%	40%

8/10 = .8 = 80%

6/10 = .6 = 60%

FIGURE A-1   PERCENTAGING A TABLE

A-2 How to Construct a Scatterplot

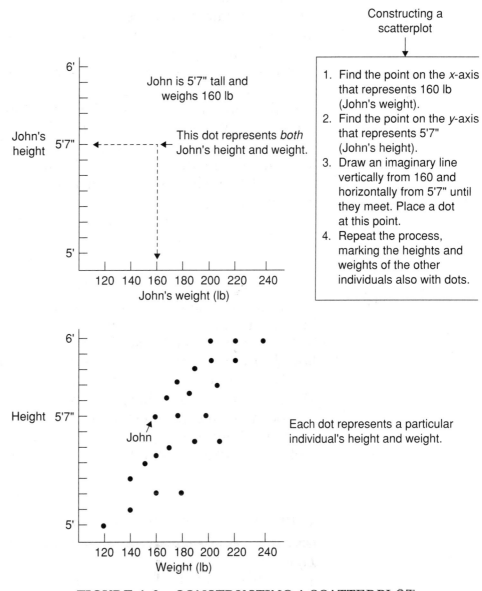

Constructing a scatterplot

1. Find the point on the x-axis that represents 160 lb (John's weight).
2. Find the point on the y-axis that represents 5'7" (John's height).
3. Draw an imaginary line vertically from 160 and horizontally from 5'7" until they meet. Place a dot at this point.
4. Repeat the process, marking the heights and weights of the other individuals also with dots.

John is 5'7" tall and weighs 160 lb

This dot represents *both* John's height and weight.

John's height

John's weight (lb)

Each dot represents a particular individual's height and weight.

Height

John

Weight (lb)

FIGURE A-2   CONSTRUCTING A SCATTERPLOT

A-3 How to Simulate an Outcome

Simulation involves using a table of random numbers (or a computer) to imitate the chance of something occurring. It is a tool that can be used to simulate many replications of an event, once we have a probability model to work with. Let us consider an example.

A newly married couple would very much like to have a baby. In particular, they want a girl. They plan to keep having children until they have a girl or until they have four children, whichever comes first. What is the probability that they will have a girl?

Two ideas apply here. Assume first that the probability of having a girl in any of the mother's births is .5 and second that the gender of each child is independent of any previously born child's gender.

Let us use the digits in a table of random numbers to simulate a child's gender as follows:

$$0, 1, 2, 3, 4 = \text{girl}$$
$$5, 6, 7, 8, 9 = \text{boy}$$

We can simulate the couple's strategy for getting a girl by reading the numbers from the table until the couple has either a girl or four children. Let's use the first line in the table. Notice that how many numbers we need to use to simulate a repetition depends on how quickly we get a girl. Let's do 15 repetitions. Out of 15 repetitions (shown here as separated by vertical lines), a girl was born 14 times. Our estimate of the probability of this strategy working, therefore, is 14/15, or .933. Unless the couple is very unlucky, their strategy should give them a girl.

TABLE A-1 A Table of Random Numbers

Line								
1	1922	6931	2553	5102	3696	8927	2719	1033
2	5458	2605	4407	2761	9333	0003	0095	0800
3	1387	6649	1482	3485	0110	3283	4751	6628
4	6746	2099	0490	0211	5291	1253	0929	1933
5	7711	4863	6382	1729	2853	8713	7510	1787
6	8162	1471	3189	9485	2544	0192	9148	9317

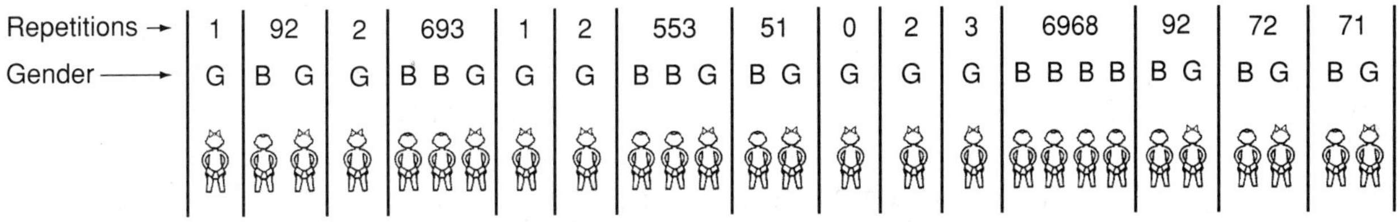

FIGURE A-3   SIMULATING AN OUTCOME

A-4 How to Read an ANOVA Table

ANOVA (analysis of variance) is a test of the statistical significance of differences in mean scores of two or more groups. The procedure requires computing an F ratio of the mean square for between groups to the mean square for within groups. Each of these mean squares is obtained by calculating a quantity called the sum of squares (SS) and dividing by the appropriate *degrees of freedom*. The F ratio is computed in Table A-2 by dividing the between groups mean square (98.3) by the within groups mean square (23.1). It is evaluated for statistical significance by using a table of F values.

In the example below, three groups are compared. The results show that the difference in means of the two groups is statistically significant at the .05 level of significance.

TABLE A-2 An ANOVA Table

Source of Variation	SS	d.f.	Mean Square	F	p
Between groups	196.6	2	98.3	4.26	<.05
Within groups	2240.7	97	23.1		
Total	2437.3	99			

(For more information about how to compute an ANOVA, see Appendix A-17.)

A-5 How to Read an ANCOVA Table

ANCOVA (analysis of covariance) is a test of the statistical significance of differences in mean scores of two or more groups while mathematically eliminating the effect of a pretest or other variable to be controlled. The procedure involves computing an F ratio of the mean square for between groups to the mean square for within groups. Each of these mean squares is obtained by calculating a quantity called sum of squares (SS) and dividing by the appropriate *degrees of freedom*. The F values are obtained by dividing the value for each of the mean squares by the value for the within mean square. The F ratio is evaluated for statistical significance by means of a table of F values.

In the example shown in Table A-3, the effects of two variables—teacher gender and teaching method along with their *interaction*—on achievement were reported. Results show that differences in teaching method had a highly significant impact on achievement ($p < .01$), whereas teacher gender had no significant effect (N.S.). The p of .06 for interaction does not reach the commonly used criterion of .05 but nonetheless suggests that further studies might find a significant interaction. The highly significant result ($p = .01$) for regression indicates that the variable controlled (a pretest) was significantly related to the achievement test scores.

TABLE A-3 An ANCOVA Table

Source of Variation	SS	d.f.	Mean Square	F	p
Between methods	1540	1	1540	25.25	<.01
Between genders	18	1	18	.30	N.S.
Interaction	231	1	231	3.79	.06
Regression	2500	1	2500	40.98	<.01
Within	5673	93	61	—	—

A-6 How to Read a Chi-Square Table

A chi-square (χ^2) table shows the values of χ^2 required for statistical significance at various degrees of freedom (d.f.). Once the appropriate d.f. have been determined and the χ^2 value has been calculated, the table indicates what the value of χ^2 must be (the "critical" value) to be considered significant at different levels of significance (e.g., .05, .01). If the calculated χ^2 value reaches or exceeds the critical χ^2 value, it is statistically significant.

For example, a χ^2 value obtained with a sample having 25 degrees of freedom must be 44.31 or higher to be statistically significant at the .01 level, as shown in Table A-4 and the curve.

TABLE A-4   Critical Region for the Chi-Square Test

Degrees of Freedom (d.f.)	Proportion in Critical Region		
	.10	.05	.01
1	2.71	3.84	6.63
2	4.61	5.99	9.21
5	9.24	11.07	15.09
10	15.99	18.31	23.21
25	34.38	37.65	44.31
50	63.17	67.50	76.15
100	118.50	124.34	135.81

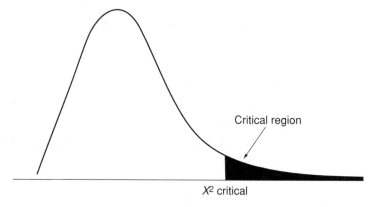

FIGURE A-4   CRITICAL REGION FOR THE CHI-SQUARE TEST

A-7 How to Read a Correlation Matrix

When correlations are computed, the results are usually reported in a table called a *correlation matrix,* which shows the correlations between all possible pairings of the variables involved. For example, Table A-5 shows the correlations between subjects' weight, arm strength, and running speed. Note the series of diagonal correlations that equal 1.00. They illustrate the fact that a variable always correlates perfectly with itself (often they are omitted, as in the upper right portion of Table A-6, because it is just a repeat of the bottom left). By studying either table, you could conclude that weight and arm strength are highly correlated, weight and running speed are negatively correlated, and there is no correlation between running speed and arm strength.

TABLE A-5 A Correlation Matrix: I

	Weight	Arm Strength	Running Speed
Weight	1.00	.85	−.58
Arm strength	.85	1.00	.03
Running speed	−.58	.03	1.00

TABLE A-6 A Correlation Matrix: II

	Weight	Arm Strength	Running Speed
Weight	—		
Arm strength	.85	—	
Running speed	−.58	.03	—

A-8 How to Read a Normal Curve Table

A normal curve table lists the areas under the normal curve that fall between and beyond various z-score values, as shown in the curve.

A portion of the normal curve table is presented in Table A-7. Column A lists the z-score values. Column B indicates the proportion of the area between a particular z-score and the mean. Column C indicates the proportion of the area that lies beyond the z-score (*Note:* Because the normal distribution is symmetrical, areas for negative z-scores are the same as those for positive z-scores).

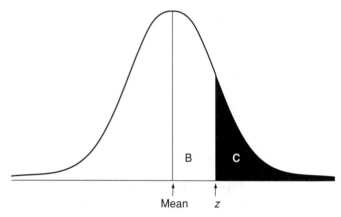

FIGURE A-5   CRITICAL REGION FOR THE NORMAL CURVE

TABLE A-7   Portion of a Normal Curve Table

A z-Score	B Area Between Mean and z	C Area Beyond z
0.00	.0000	.5000
0.25	.0987	.4013
0.50	.1915	.3085
1.00	.3413	.1587
1.50	.4332	.0668
1.96	.4750	.0250
2.00	.4772	.0228
2.50	.4938	.0062
2.58	.4951	.0049
3.00	.4987	.0013
3.50	.4998	.0002
4.00	.49997	.00003

A-9 How to Read a t Table

A *t* table shows the values of *t* required for statistical significance at various degrees of freedom (d.f.). Once the appropriate d.f. have been determined and the *t* value has been calculated, the table indicates what the calculated *t* value must be (the critical *t* value) to be considered statistically significant at different levels of significance (e.g., .25, .05, .01).

For example, a *t* value calculated for a sample having 10 d.f. in a one-tailed test must be at least 1.812 to be considered statistically significant at the .05 level, as shown in Table A-8 and the curve.

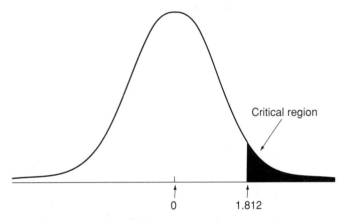

FIGURE A-6   CRITICAL REGION FOR THE *t*-TEST

TABLE A-8   Portion of a *t* Table

Degrees of Freedom	Proportion in Critical Region			
	.40	.10	.05	.01
1	0.325	3.078	6.314	31.821
5	0.267	1.476	2.015	3.365
10	0.260	1.372	1.812	2.764
25	0.256	1.316	1.708	2.485
40	0.255	1.303	1.684	2.423
60	0.254	1.296	1.671	2.390

A-10 How to Read an F Table

An *F* table shows the values required for statistical significance at various degrees of freedom (d.f.). In this case, the d.f. must be determined for the values in both the numerator and denominator of the *F* ratio. Once the appropriate d.f. and the *F* value have been calculated (in ANOVA or ANCOVA), the table indicates what the calculated *F* value must be (the "critical" *F* value) to be considered statistically significant at different levels of significance (usually, only the .05 and .01 levels are shown).

For example, an *F* value calculated for a sample having 7 d.f. in the numerator and 10 d.f. in the denominator must be at least 3.14 to be considered statistically significant at the .05 level, as shown in the curve in Figure A-7.

TABLE A-9   Portion of an *F* Table

Degrees of Freedom in Denominator	Degrees of Freedom in Numerator								
	1	**2**	**3**	**4**	**5**	**7**	**10**	**16**	**20**
10	4.96	4.10	3.71	3.48	3.33	3.14	2.97	2.82	2.77
	10.04	**7.56**	**6.55**	**5.99**	**5.64**	**5.21**	**4.85**	**4.52**	**4.41**
20	4.35	3.49	3.10	2.87	2.71	2.52	2.35	2.18	2.12
	8.10	**5.85**	**4.94**	**4.43**	**4.10**	**3.71**	**3.37**	**3.05**	**2.94**
50	4.03	3.18	2.79	2.56	2.40	2.20	2.02	1.85	1.78
	7.17	**5.06**	**4.20**	**3.72**	**3.41**	**3.02**	**2.70**	**2.39**	**2.26**
100	3.94	3.09	2.70	2.46	2.30	2.10	1.92	1.75	1.68
	6.90	**4.82**	**3.98**	**3.51**	**3.20**	**2.82**	**2.51**	**2.19**	**2.06**
400	3.86	3.02	2.62	2.39	2.23	2.03	1.85	1.67	1.60
	6.70	**4.66**	**3.83**	**3.36**	**3.06**	**2.69**	**2.37**	**2.04**	**1.92**

Note: Entries in lightface type are critical values at the .05 level; those in boldface type are critical values at the .01 level.

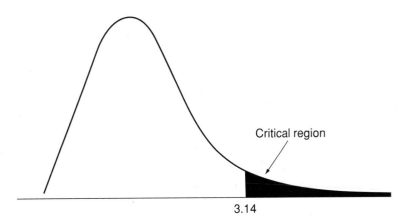

Critical region

3.14

FIGURE A-7   CRITICAL REGION FOR THE *F*-TEST

A-11 How to Read a Significance Table for the Pearson Correlation

This statistical table shows the values that a correlation coefficient must reach or exceed to be considered statistically significant at various degrees of freedom (d.f.). Once the appropriate d.f. ($n - 2$) have been determined and the correlation coefficient has been calculated, the table indicates what the correlation must be (the critical value) to be considered statistically significant at different levels of significance (e.g., .05, .01), and for either a one- or two-tailed test.

For example, a correlation coefficient calculated for a sample with a 20 d.f. must be at least .423 to be statistically significant at the .05 level for a two-tailed test.

TABLE A-10 Portion of a Pearson *r* Table

	Level of Significance for One-Tailed Test			
	.05	**.025**	**.01**	**.005**
	Level of Significance for Two-Tailed Test			
d.f.	**.10**	**.05**	**.02**	**.01**
1	.988	.997	.9995	.9999
5	.669	.754	.833	.874
10	.497	.576	.658	.708
15	.412	.482	.558	.606
20	.360	.423	.492	.537
50	.231	.273	.322	.354
100	.164	.195	.230	.254

A-12 How to Draw a Regression Line

The general formula for the regression equation for predicting y values from x values is $y' = a + bx$. In this formula, a and b are constants and y' is the predicted value for the y variable corresponding to a particular value on the x variable.

To plot a regression line, the constants a and b must be determined from statistical values computed from the data. They include the standard deviation of the x values, the standard deviation of the y values, and the Pearson correlation coefficient. For the sake of brevity, the arithmetic of the computations is not shown here, but the formulas are very simple. They can be found in any elementary statistics book (see the bibliography).

For the example that follows, suppose that the constants a and b were obtained from the data for the scatterplot shown in Figure A-8. The data were scores of a sample of 15 fourth-grade students on both a reading test and a spelling test.[1] The computed value for a was 2.29 and b was 0.72. The regression equation, therefore, would be $y' = 2.29 + 0.72x$. The steps involved in plotting the regression line, then, would be as follows:

1. Pick a relatively low value on the independent (the predictor) variable x (let's use the reading score of 2), and substitute it for x in the regression equation. Solve for y'. The answer is $y' = 3.73$. This is the predicted score on the dependent (spelling) variable.
2. Plot the point for a reading score of $x = 2$ and a predicted spelling score of $y' = 3.73$ on the scatterplot.
3. Now pick a rather high reading score (let's use a 9) for the x value in this example, and then substitute it in the regression equation and, again, solve for y'. The answer is $y' = 8.77$; this is the predicted spelling score.
4. Plot a second point on the scatterplot for a reading score of $x = 9$ and a predicted spelling score of $y' = 8.77$.
5. Draw a straight line through both of these points. This line is the regression line.

---

[1] Ordinarily, a larger sample is used in applications of regression methods, but a sample of 15 is sufficient to illustrate the procedures involved in drawing the regression line.

It is a good idea to check your work by picking an additional value for *x*, using the regression equation to compute the *y′* value for a third point, and then plotting it on the scatterplot. If it does not fall on the regression line that connects the other two points, a mistake has been made in computing the values for at least one of the three points (This accuracy check was done for an *x* value of 6 on the reading test, with *y′* = 6.61. Note that this point falls on the regression line.)

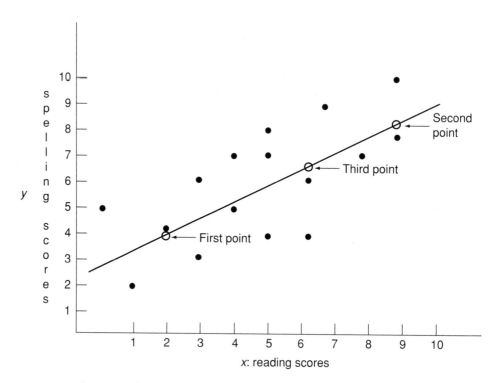

FIGURE A-8   SCATTERPLOT AND THE REGRESSION LINE FOR PREDICTING SPELLING SCORES FROM READING SCORES

A-13 How to Calculate a Correlation Coefficient

Actually, there are many different correlation coefficients, each applying to a particular circumstance and each calculated by a different computational formula. The one we describe here is the one most frequently used: the Pearson product-moment coefficient of correlation. It is symbolized by the lowercase letter r.

A correlation coefficient expresses the relationship between two quantitative variables in numerical terms. When the data for both variables involve interval or ratio data, the Pearson r is the appropriate correlation coefficient to calculate. The formula for calculating the Pearson r coefficient is

$$r = \frac{n\Sigma XY - (\Sigma X)(\Sigma Y)}{\sqrt{[n\Sigma X^2 - (\Sigma X)^2][n\Sigma Y^2 - (\Sigma Y)^2]}}$$

The Pearson formula looks a lot more complicated than it really is. It does have a lot of steps to follow before we finally get to the end, but as you will see, each step is easy to calculate. Let's give it a try.

Imagine that we have the numbers of radios and clocks possessed by people living in six different homes. What we would like to know is whether these two variables (number of clocks and number of radios) are related, and if so, how—positively? negatively? To

TABLE A-11   Clocks versus Radios

Family Name	Number of Clocks (X)	Number of Radios (Y)
Jones	3	2
Chung	6	6
Johnson	5	7
Okuda	2	5
Patton	6	7
Berkowitz	2	3

answer these questions, we apply the Pearson formula and calculate the correlation coefficient for the two sets of numbers.

As you can see in Table A-12, ΣX equals the sum of the numbers in the X column, that is, the total number of clocks. ΣY equals the sum of the numbers in the Y column, that is, the total number of radios. ΣX^2 equals the sum of the squares of each of the numbers in the X column. ΣY^2 equals the sum of the squares of each of the numbers in the Y column. ΣXY equals the sum of the products of the X and Y scores (i.e., the sum of each X score multiplied by its corresponding Y score). Now we simply substitute each of these sums into the formula as shown below:

$$r = \frac{6(135) - (24)(30)}{\sqrt{[6(114) - (24)^2][6(172) - (30)^2]}}$$

The n in the formula simply refers to the number of *pairs* of scores there are (six in this example). To determine r, we now perform the following calculations:

1. First, multiply ΣXY by n: $135(6) = 810$.
2. Multiply ΣX by ΣY: $24(30) = 720$.
3. Subtract step 2 from step 1: $810 - 720 = 90$.
4. Multiply ΣX^2 by n: $114(6) = 684$.
5. Square ΣX: $(24)^2 = 576$.
6. Subtract step 5 from step 4: $684 - 576 = 108$.
7. Multiply ΣY^2 by n: $172(6) = 1032$.
8. Square ΣY: $(30)^2 = 900$
9. Subtract step 8 from step 7: $1032 - 900 = 132$.
10. Multiply step 6 by step 9: $108(132) = 14256$.
11. Take the square root of step 10: $14256 = 119.4$
12. Divide step 3 by step 11: $90/119.4 = r = .75$

TABLE A-12   Clocks versus Radios Revisited

Family Name	Number of Clocks (X)	Number of Radios (Y)	X^2	Y^2	XY
Jones	3	2	9	4	6
Chung	6	6	36	36	36
Johnson	5	7	25	49	35
Okuda	2	5	4	25	10
Patton	6	7	36	49	42
Berkowitz	2	3	4	9	6
Totals ⟶	24	30	114	172	135
	↑ ΣX	↑ ΣY	↑ ΣX^2	↑ ΣY^2	↑ ΣXY

A-14 How to Calculate a Standard Deviation

There is a need for measures that describe the *spread,* or *variability,* that exists within distributions. By far, the most useful index of variability is the **standard deviation (SD)** of a distribution. The formula for calculating the standard deviation is

$$SD = \sqrt{\frac{\Sigma(X - \bar{X})^2}{n}}$$

Every score in the distribution is used to calculate it.

Suppose we have the five test scores shown in Table A-13:

ΣX = the sum of the numbers in the X column (the test scores); $\Sigma(X - \bar{X})^2$ = the sum of each score minus the mean, which is then squared. The steps involved in calculating the SD are straightforward:

1. Calculate the mean of the distribution: $\bar{X} = \Sigma X/n = 30/5 = 6$.
2. Subtract the mean from each score (Symbolized by $X - \bar{X}$). For example, $9 - 6 = 3$.
3. Square each of these differences $(X - \bar{X})^2$. For example, $3^2 = 9$.
4. Add up the squares of these differences $\Sigma(X - \bar{X})^2 = 26$.
5. Divide the total by the number of scores: $26/5 = 5.2$. The result is called the **variance.**
6. Take the square root of the variance: $\sqrt{5.2} = 2.28$. This is the standard deviation.

TABLE A-13   Calculation of the Standard Deviation of a Distribution

Test Score (X)	Mean ($\bar{X}$)	($X - \bar{X}$)	($X - \bar{X}$)^2
9	6	3	9
8	6	2	4
6	6	0	0
4	6	-2	4
3	6	-3	9
$\Sigma = 30$			$\Sigma = 26$

You should notice that the more spread out the scores in a distribution are, the larger will be the standard deviation. The closer the scores are to the mean, the less spread out they are and hence the smaller the standard deviation. Thus, if we were describing two sets of scores on the same test and we found that the standard deviation for the scores in one set was 3.2, while the standard deviation for the other set was 10.1, we would know that there was much less variability in the first set—that is, the scores were closer together.

A-15 How to Perform a Chi-Square Test

Chi-square is the most commonly used statistic for determining whether a relationship between two categorical variables is statistically significant (i.e., not attributable to chance). It is also the first step involved in calculating the contingency coefficient—an index of the *degree* of relationship that exists. The formula for calculating chi-square is

$$\chi^2 = \sum \frac{(f_o - f_e)^2}{f_e}$$

As is so often the case, this formula is much easier to use than might first appear. Here is an example. Suppose we wish to determine whether, in a particular area, there is a relationship between size of city and the relative number of chain restaurants compared to non-chain restaurants in the city. The data might look like that in Table A-14.

TABLE A-14 Number of Chain Compared to Non-Chain Restaurants in Different Cities: I

City	Number of Non-Chain Restaurants	Number of Chain Restaurants
A	70	30
B	130	70
C	160	140

Each number represents the number of either chain or non-chain restaurants that are to be found in cities A, B, and C. These are the *observed* frequencies (f_o).

Now, to obtain χ^2, we proceed through the following steps, as shown in Table A-15:

1. Add up (total) all of the columns (chain and non-chain) and rows (Cities A, B, and C). For example, the total number of non-chain restaurants is 360.

TABLE A-15 Number of Chain Compared to Non-Chain Restaurants in Different Cities: II

City	Number of Non-Chain Restaurants	Number of Chain Restaurants	Totals
A	70 (60)	30 (40)	100
B	130 (120)	70 (80)	200
C	160 (180)	140 (120)	300
Totals $\longrightarrow$	360	240	600

2. Calculate the proportion of the total frequency that falls in each row (or column). Thus, we see that City A has 100/600, or 1/6 of the total number of restaurants. City B has 200/600, or 1/3 of the total. City C has 300/600, or 1/2 of the total.

3. Multiply each row proportion by its column total. These are the *expected* frequencies (f_e). For City A, the f_e for non-chains is 1/6(360), or 60. For chains, it is 1/6(240), or 40. These values are shown in parentheses in the table.

4. For each cell, subtract the expected frequency (f_e) from the obtained frequency (f_o), square the result, and then divide it by f_e. The results in this example are as follows:

$$\frac{(70 - 60)^2}{(60)} = \frac{10^2}{60} = \frac{100}{60} = 1.67$$

$$\frac{(30 - 40)^2}{(40)} = \frac{-10^2}{40} = \frac{100}{40} = 2.50$$

$$\frac{(130 - 120)^2}{(120)} = \frac{10^2}{120} = \frac{100}{120} = 0.83$$

$$\frac{(70 - 80)^2}{(80)} = \frac{-10^2}{80} = \frac{100}{80} = 1.25$$

$$\frac{(160 - 180)^2}{(180)} = \frac{-20^2}{180} = \frac{400}{180} = 2.2$$

$$\frac{(140 - 120)^2}{120} = \frac{20^2}{120} = \frac{400}{120} = 3.33$$

5. Add these six values symbolized by

$$\sum \frac{(f_o - f_e)^2}{fe}$$

to obtain chi-square. Thus, $\chi^2 = 11.80$.

To determine statistical significance, the calculated value of χ^2 is compared to values in a chi-square table. Reading the table requires that one first calculate the appropriate number of degrees of freedom. For a table having "r" rows and "c" columns, d.f. = $(r - 1)(c - 1)$. Table A-14 has three rows and two columns, so d.f. = $(3 - 1) \times (2 - 1) = 2$. A chi-square table indicates that, with 2 d.f., a value of 5.99 is required for a result to be statistically significant at the .05 level. The value of 11.80 we obtained, therefore, *would* be statistically significant.

The formula for the contingency coefficient (C) is:

$$C = \sqrt{\frac{\chi^2}{\chi^2 + n}}$$

where n = total number of cases
$\sqrt{}$ = square root

Thus, in the above example, $\chi^2 = 11.80$ and $n = 600$.

$$C = \sqrt{\frac{11.80}{11.80 + 600}} = \sqrt{\frac{11.80}{611.80}} = \sqrt{.02} = .14$$

Note: The maximum value for C depends on the number of rows and columns that exist in a particular instance. In this case, the maximum number for a 2×3 table (2 columns, 3 rows) is approximately .76. Our obtained value of .14 indicates only a slight relationship.

A-16 How to Perform a *t*-Test for Independent Means

A *t*-test for independent means is the most commonly used index for determining whether the difference in means between two independent (i.e., uncorrelated) groups of scores is statistically significant (i.e., not attributable to chance). The formula used is:

$$t = \frac{\overline{X}_1 - \overline{X}_2}{\sqrt{\dfrac{s^2}{n_1} + \dfrac{s^2}{n_2}}}$$

TABLE A-16   Inches of Rainfall in Two Cities

Day	City A	City B
Monday	1	0
Tuesday	3	4
Wednesday	0	5
Thursday	3	6
Friday	5	3
Saturday	2	2
Sunday	0	1

Here is an example. Suppose the inches of rainfall for two cities during the same week are those shown in Table A-16.

The necessary computations begin as in Table A-17.

1. Calculate the average number of inches of rainfall per day for each city: $\overline{X} = \dfrac{\Sigma X}{n}$, where $\overline{X}$ stands for the mean, ΣX indicates the sum of the inches of rainfall in each city, and n is the total number of days. Thus,

TABLE A-17   Daily Inches of Rainfall in Two Cities

	City A			City B		
Day	X_1	$X_1 - \bar{X}_1$	$(X_1 - \bar{X}_1)^2$	X_2	$X_2 - \bar{X}_2$	$(X_2 - \bar{X}_2)^2$
Monday	1	−1	1	0	−3	9
Tuesday	3	+1	1	4	+1	1
Wednesday	0	−2	4	5	+2	4
Thursday	3	+1	1	6	+3	9
Friday	5	+3	9	3	0	0
Saturday	2	0	0	2	−1	1
Sunday	0	−2	4	1	−2	4
Total	14		20	21		28
	↑		↑	↑		↑
	ΣX_1		$\Sigma(X_1 - \bar{X}_1)^2$	ΣX_2		$\Sigma(X_2 - \bar{X}_2)^2$

$$\bar{X}_1 = \frac{\Sigma X_1}{n_1} = \frac{14}{7} = 2 \qquad \bar{X}_2 = \frac{\Sigma X_2}{n_2} = \frac{21}{7} = 3$$

2. For each city, subtract the mean from each day's inches of rainfall and then square this difference. The sum of these squared differences gives us $\Sigma(X_1 - \bar{X}_1)^2 = 20$, and $\Sigma(X_2 - \bar{X}_2)^2 = 28$.
3. Obtain s^2 as follows:

$$s^2 = \frac{\Sigma(X_1 - \bar{X}_1)^2 + \Sigma(X_2 - \bar{X}_2)^2}{n_1 + n_2 - 2} = \frac{20 + 28}{7 + 7 - 2} = \frac{48}{12} = 4.00$$

4. Calculate t, using the formula given earlier:

$$t = \frac{\bar{X}_1 - \bar{X}_2}{\sqrt{\dfrac{s^2}{n_1} + \dfrac{s^2}{n_2}}} = \frac{2.0 - 3.0}{\sqrt{\dfrac{4.00}{7} + \dfrac{4.00}{7}}} = \frac{-1.0}{\sqrt{.57 + .57}} = \frac{-1.0}{\sqrt{1.14}} = \frac{-1.0}{1.06} = -.94$$

5. Finally, compare the obtained t-value (.94) with the values in a t table (similar to the one shown in Appendix A-10) to determine whether it is statistically significant. A t value calculated for a sample having 12 degrees of freedom with a 2-tailed test (in this case, $n_1 + n_2 - 2 = 7 + 7 - 2 = 12$) must be at least 2.18 to be considered statistically significant at the .05 level. Since .94 is much smaller than 2.18, we conclude that the obtained difference in means of 1.0 is *not* statistically significant, but instead just a chance result.

A-17 How to Calculate a One-Way Analysis of Variance

Analysis of variance (ANOVA) is the procedure that is most commonly used for determining the statistical significance of differences among means for multiple groups (although it can also be used with only two groups, in which case it is equivalent to the t-test). Let us consider an example.

Suppose we have as initial data the number of identified archeological ruins per section (square mile) for random samples of five sections from each of three national forests. These data are shown in Table A-18.

The necessary computations begin as shown in Table A-18.

TABLE A-18 Identified Ruins in Three Forests

Forest I	Forest II	Forest III	
X_1	X_2	X_3	
5	2	7	
8	3	2	
3	1	5	
2	3	3	
7	6	3	
$n = 5$	$n = 5$	$n = 5$	
$\Sigma X_1 = 25$	$\Sigma X_2 = 15$	$\Sigma X_3 = 20$	$= \Sigma\Sigma X = 60$
$\Sigma X_1^2 = 151$	$\Sigma X_2^2 = 59$	$\Sigma X_3^2 = 96$	$= \Sigma\Sigma X^2 = 306$
$(\Sigma X_1)^2 = 625$	$(\Sigma X_2)^2 = 225$	$(\Sigma X_3)^2 = 400$	$= \Sigma(\Sigma X)^2 = 1250$

1. Add the numbers for each forest to get the sum (Σ) of each (e.g., $\Sigma X_1 = 25$).
2. Square each of the numbers for each forest and then sum these squares. Thus, for Forest I, we have $(5^2 + 8^2 + 3^2 + 2^2 + 7^2) = (25 + 64 + 9 + 4 + 49) = 151$.
3. Take the sum for each forest and square it. For Forest I, this gives us $25^2 = 625$.
4. Now, sum across forests. Thus, $\Sigma X_1 + \Sigma X_2 + \Sigma X_3 = 60$; $\Sigma X_1^2 + \Sigma X_2^2 + \Sigma X_3^2 = 306$; and $(\Sigma X_1^2) + (\Sigma X_2^2) + (\Sigma X_3^2) = 1250$.
5. These values are now substituted into three equations to obtain three new values entitled "between sum of squares," "within sum of squares" and "total sum of squares" as follows where G = number of groups (in this case 3 forests) and n is the number of scores in each group (in this case $n = 5$)

$$between\ sum\ of\ squares = \frac{1}{nG}\left[G\Sigma(\Sigma X)^2 - (\Sigma\Sigma X)^2\right]$$

This gives $= \frac{1}{(5)(3)}\left[3(1250) - 60^2\right] = \frac{1}{15}\left[3750 - 3600\right] = \frac{1}{15}(150) = 10.0$

$$Total\ sum\ of\ squares = \frac{1}{nG}\left[nG\Sigma\Sigma X^2 - (\Sigma\Sigma X)^2\right]$$

This gives $= \frac{1}{(5)(3)}\left[(15)(306) - 60^2\right] = \frac{1}{15}\left[4590 - 3600\right] = \frac{1}{15}(990) = 66.0$

$$within\ sum\ of\ squares = \frac{1}{n}\left[n\Sigma\Sigma X^2 - \Sigma(\Sigma X)^2\right]$$

This gives $= \frac{1}{5}\left[5(306) - 1250\right] = \frac{1}{5}\left[1530 - 1250\right] = \frac{1}{5}(280) = 56.0$

Notice that the *between sum of squares* and *within sum of squares* must add up to the *total sum of squares*. We see that is the case here $(10 + 56 = 66)$.

6. We now enter these values for sum of squares into an ANOVA table (see A-19).

Statistical significance in this example is determined by comparing the obtained value of *F* with a table of *F* values (similar to the one shown in Appendix A-10). An *F*-value calculated for a sample having 2 degrees of freedom in the numerator and 12 degrees of freedom in the denominator (as obtained here) must be at least 3.88 to be considered statistically significant at the .05 level of significance. Since our obtained value of 1.06 is much lower than 3.88, it is *not* statistically significant at the .05 level.

TABLE A-19 An ANOVA Table

Source of Variation	SS	d.f.	Mean Square	F	p
Between groups	10.0	2	5.0	1.06	N.S.
Within groups	56.0	12	4.7		
Total	66.0	14			

Bibliography

Freedman, David, et al. (1991). *Statistics*. New York: W. W. Norton.

Gonick, Larry and Woollcott Smith. (1993). *The cartoon guide to statistics*. New York: HarperCollins.

Graham, Alan. (1993). *Teach yourself statistics*. Chicago: NTC Publishing Group.

Grimm, Laurence C. (1993). *Statistical applications for the behavioral sciences*. New York: John Wiley & Sons.

Holcomb, Zealure C. (1998). *Fundamentals of descriptive statistics*. Los Angeles: Pyrczak.

Huff, Darrell. (1982). *How to lie with statistics*. New York: W. W. Norton.

Iman, Ronald L. (1995). *A data-based approach to statistics*. San Francisco: Duxbury Press.

Knapp, Thomas R. (1996). *Learning statistics through playing cards*. Thousand Oaks, CA: Sage.

Koosis, Donald J. (1997). *Statistics: A self-teaching guide*. (4th ed.). New York: John Wiley & Sons.

Moore, David S. (1995). *The basic practice of statistics*. New York: W. H. Freeman.

Moore, David S. (1997). *Statistics: Concepts and controversies*. (4th ed.). New York: W. H. Freeman.

Phillips, John L. (1996). *How to think about statistics*. New York: W. H. Freeman.

Pyrczak, Fred. (1995). *Making sense of statistics: A conceptual overview*. Los Angeles: Pyrczak.

Rowntree, Derek. (1984). *Probability without tears*. New York: Barnes & Noble.

Sheskin, David J. (Ed.) (1997). *Handbook of parametric and non-parametric statistical procedures*. New York: CRC Press.

Shiffer, Ronald E.L., and Arthur J. Adams. (1996). *Just the basics, please: A quick review of math for introductory statistics*. Belmont, CA: Duxbury Press.

Utts, Jessica M. (1996). *Seeing through statistics*. San Francisco: Duxbury Press.

Wallgren, Anders et al. (1996). *Graphing statistics and data: Creating better charts*. Newbury Park, CA: Sage.

Weaver, Jefferson H. (1997). *Conquering statistics: Numbers without the crunch*. New York: Plenum Trade.

Witte, Robert S. (1989). *Statistics*. (3rd ed.). San Francisco: Holt, Rinehart & Winston.

Glossary[*]

Abscissa The distance from the y-axis to a point on a graph with rectangular coordinates, measured along the x-axis. See **x-y axes** concept.

Alternative hypothesis The opposite of null hypothesis. In a test for statistical significance of differences between means, it is a statement that there is a difference in means in the population.

ANCOVA Acronym for *analysis of covariance*. See **analysis of covariance** concept.

ANOVA Acronym for *analysis of variance*. See **analysis of variance** concept.

A posteriori tests Tests for statistical significance conducted after analysis of variance is completed to determine which particular pairs of means differ significantly.

A priori tests Comparisons that are planned before conducting an analysis of variance to determine which particular pairs of means differ sufficiently for the result to be statistically significant.

Arithmetic average Same as the mean. It is the sum of a set of numbers divided by the number of numbers in the set. See **mean** concept.

Average A general term for a variety of measures of central tendency, i.e., of the middle point in a distribution.

[*]These are additional concepts or terms that are mentioned in our discussions and descriptions throughout the text but not described or explained in detail.

Bayesian statistics   A branch of statistics in which probabilities are first estimated subjectively, then revised as additional information becomes available. See **subjective probability** concept.

Bell-shaped curve   A graph representing the probabilities of a normal distribution. See **normal distribution** concept.

Best-fitting line   The line in a correlation scatterplot that is closest to all of the plots according to some criterion. See **least squares criterion (or principle)** concept.

Between variance estimate   The estimate of the population variance in analysis of variance based on the differences among the means of the groups involved. See **analysis of variance** concept.

Box-and-whiskers diagram   A figure that shows graphically a summary of the main characteristics of a distribution. See **boxplot** concept.

Case An individual (or object) on whom information has been collected on one or more variables.

Cause-and-effect relationship   A relationship between one or more variables such that variation in one or more of them brings about a change in one or more of the other variables. See **correlation versus causation** concept.

Central tendency   A clustering of the measurements in a distribution about a particular point in the distribution. See **mean, median,** and **mode** concepts.

Coefficient of multiple determination   In multiple correlation, the coefficient of multiple determination is a numerical index that indicates how much the variations in the predictor variables determine or explain the variation in the predicted variable. See **coefficient of determination** and **multiple correlation** concepts.

Comparison group   A sample in a research project that does not receive the experimental treatment or that has had experiences different from the sample that is the focus of the investigation.

Computational formula   A statistical formula that, in contrast to a definitional formula, is structured for ease of calculation, rather than for revealing the basic meaning or rationale of the statistic represented by the formula.

Correlated samples design   A research design in which there is some kind of relationship between the samples. An example would be a study of twins in which one member of each pair of twins is in one group and the other member is in the other group. See **matched pairs design** concept.

Counts   Procedures in which individuals or objects that fit a category are counted and recorded for analysis.

Criterion-referenced test A test in which the instrument is designed to indicate whether the individual responding to the test has met a particular standard or criterion—as contrasted to a norm-referenced test, which yields a score that indicates the individual's relative position in a group.

Curvilinear relationship A pattern of plots in a correlation scatterplot that fits a curve rather than a straight line. See **correlation ratio** concept.

Definitional formula A statistical formula that represents the basic meaning or rationale of the statistical concept directly—unlike a computational formula, which is structured for computational efficiency.

Dichotomous variable A basis for classification in which individuals or objects are to be placed in only one of two mutually exclusive categories.

Direct correlation Another name for positive correlation. See **positive correlation** concept.

Dispersion The extent to which a set of measurements are widely scattered or closely bunched together. See **range, interquartile range**, and **standard deviation** concepts.

Distribution curve A graph that represents the frequencies as in a frequency polygon except that a smoothed line is drawn through the plots instead of connecting the dots with straight lines. See **frequency polygon** and **normal distribution** concepts.

Expected frequency In chi-square analysis, the expected frequencies are the frequencies implied by the null hypothesis. Also known as *theoretical frequencies*. See **chi-square** concept.

Factorial design A research design involving analysis of variance that makes it possible to simultaneously study the effects of two or more independent variables on a dependent variable separately and also of the effects of their interaction. See **analysis of variance** concept.

***F* ratio, *F* value** The quotient obtained by dividing the larger estimate of the population variance by the smaller estimate. For example, in one-way analysis of variance, the variance estimate based on differences among the means is divided by the variance estimate based on the variance within groups.

Frequency The number of times a certain event occurred, or the number of times a given number appears in a set of numbers. See **Appendix A-15: How to Perform a Chi-Square Test**.

Homogeneous Similar in characteristics, with only a small amount of variability from individual to individual in a group or from object to object in a set of objects.

Hypothesis of uniform distribution The type of hypothesis sometimes used in the chi-square test of goodness of fit when the null hypothesis requires that all of the expected frequencies have the same value. See **chi-square** concept.

Inclusive range The difference between the highest measurement and the lowest measurement in a distribution plus 1, as contrasted with the commonly used procedure of simply using the difference between the highest and lowest values.

Inference A judgment or conclusion based on data or logical premises.

Infinite A quantity with no limit that gets larger and larger beyond any number that has been assigned previously.

Intercorrelated A relationship between or among two or more variables that are either directly (positively) or inversely (negatively) correlated with each other. See **positive correlation** and **negative correlation** concepts.

Interval estimate A procedure through which a probability statement can be made, based on sample data, regarding the likelihood that the true population value is within a computed range of values. See **confidence interval** concept.

Interval size The difference between the upper and lower limits of a class interval when measurements are grouped in intervals that are one or more units in width on the scale of measurement. See **class interval** and **grouped frequency distribution** concepts.

Inverse correlation Same as negative correlation. See **negative correlation** concept.

Leptokurtic The shape of a frequency curve that is more peaked than the normal distribution curve.

Levels of treatment The different kinds of treatments in an experiment, or the different amounts of something given to different treatment groups, for example, differences in the size of the dosages given to subjects in different groups in an experiment on effects of a new medication.

Limited range problem Same as restricted range effect. A difficulty in interpreting correlation coefficients when based on a sample that is more homogeneous than the population to which inferences will be made based on the sample data. See **restricted range effect** concept.

Linear relation A relationship such that an increase (or decrease) in one variable is accompanied by a proportionate increase (or decrease) in the other variable. The plots in a scatterplot cluster around a straight line with such a relationship. See **regression line** concept.

Lower real limit The low end of a class interval. See **class interval** concept.

Lurking variable   Same as extraneous variable. See **extraneous variable** concept.

MANOVA   Acronym for *multivariate analysis of variance*. See **multivariate analysis of variance** concept.

Marginal totals   The row totals and column totals in a cross-break table or correlation scatterplot.

Matched subjects design   Same as matched pairs design. See **matched pairs design** concept.

Mean square   Another name for estimate of population variance.

Measurement error   Variations in the measurements on the same individual or object—all obtained with the same instrument.

Mu (μ)   A Greek letter, often used as the symbol for population mean.

Multiple regression   A regression method that makes it possible to predict values on a dependent variable on the basis of known values of two or more independent (predictor) variables.

Negative skewness   The shape of a graph of a distribution when the high concentration of measurements is near the high end of the scale with the infrequent measurements extending toward the low end. See **skewed distribution** concept.

Norm-referenced test   A test designed to provide scores that indicate where an individual stands in relation to other members of a group. See **norm** concept.

N.S.   Abbreviation for *not (statistically) significant*.

Nuisance variable   Another name for extraneous variable. See **extraneous variable** concept.

Objectivity   The extent to which an observer is able to make and record observations with the least possible influence by his or her expectations, preferences, biases, or other characteristics as an observer. Also, the extent to which a measuring instrument can be used with the least possible influence on the scores by expectations, and so forth, of the people who administer and score the instrument.

Observation   Use of one or more of the five senses to obtain and record information on individuals, objects or events.

Observed frequency   In chi-square analysis, an actual count of the number of individuals or objects in a particular category. See chi-square concept.

Ordinate   The distance from the *x*-axis to a point on a graph with rectangular coordinates, measured along the *y*-axis. See ***x-y* axes** and **scatterplot** concepts.

Origin   In Cartesian coordinates, the intersection of the *x*-axis and the *y*-axis. It is the zero point on both the horizontal and vertical axes. See ***x-y* axes** concept.

Outcome variable Another name for *dependent variable*. See **dependent/independent variables** concept.

Pair differences The differences between the measurements for the members of each pair of subjects in a variety of kinds of paired comparisons.

Pilot study A small-scale, exploratory study conducted before a larger study to identify possible weaknesses in the design and to identify problems that should be anticipated.

Platykurtic The shape of a distribution curve that is flatter (less peaked) than the bell-shaped normal distribution curve.

Pooled estimate The best approximation possible of the value of a population parameter, such a *variance*, based on measurements obtained on two or more samples. See **Appendix A-16: How to Perform a *t*-Test**.

Population parameter A true value or measurement of a characteristic of an entire population, such as a mean, or a standard deviation. Can be estimated only in studies based on samples. See **statistic/parameter** concept.

Positive skewness The shape of a distribution when the high concentration of measurements is near the low end of the scale with the infrequent measurements extending toward the high end. See **skewed distribution** concept.

Post hoc tests Tests of statistical significance that are used after an analysis of variance involving three or more groups is completed. The purpose is to determine which particular pairs of means differ sufficiently for the differences to be statistically significant.

Posttest The second test administered in a before-and-after comparison intended to measure change in achievement, attitude, and so forth. (The *first* test given is called a pretest.)

Practical significance See substantive significance.

Prediction equation An equation used in prediction studies. One kind of prediction equation is a regression equation. See **regression equation** concept.

Predictor variable The variable used in estimating values on another variable in prediction studies. See **regression equation** concept.

Pretest The first test administered in a before-and-after comparison intended to measure change in achievement, attitude, and so forth. (The *second* test is called a posttest.)

Probability model A theoretical formulation such as the normal distribution table, or the binomial distribution, that provides a basis for determining probabilities. See **Appendix A-3: How to Simulate an Outcome**.

Proportion   A decimal fraction that is obtained by dividing the number of individuals, objects, or events having a certain characteristic by the total number of individuals, objects, or events involved. See **pie chart** and **percentage/proportion** concepts.

Questionnaire   Usually a written instrument with questions that the respondent is to answer either by marking certain choices or by recording handwritten answers. Guidesheets that interviewers use are also sometimes called questionnaires.

Random assignment   The process of placing individuals or objects in groups on the basis of pure chance, such as use of a table of random numbers. See **matched pairs design** concept.

Range of talent problem   Same as restricted range effect. A difficulty in interpreting correlation coefficients based on a sample that is more homogeneous than the population to which inferences will be made based on the sample data. See **restricted range effect** concept.

Rank, rank order   An arrangement of individuals, objects, or ideas in a sequence based on some criterion such as level of achievement, quality, time of arrival, and so forth, using numbers to indicate which are first, second, third, and so on. See **ordinal scale** concept.

Rating scale   An instrument used in evaluating individuals, objects, performances, and so forth. Contains scales for descriptions of characteristics, such as behaviors, achievements, and so forth. The rater is asked to place marks on the scales to indicate degree of excellence, level of quality and so forth. The numbers marked on the scales are usually summed to obtain a total score.

Raw score   The original score obtained from a test or other measuring instrument before being modified by any kind of statistical treatment.

Reciprocal causal relation   A relationship between two influences in which each brings about a change in the other that results in a cumulative increase, or decrease, in both variables. See **correlation versus causation** concept for examples.

Related samples design   A plan for research in which there is some kind of similarity or relationship among the groups involved. Examples are one group made up of fathers and the other composed of their sons, young men in one group and their girlfriends in the other, and matched pair designs in which each pair member is assigned to one group and the other member to the other group.

Replication   Repetition of a study, preferably with different samples and conducted by different researchers. The purpose is to determine whether the conclusions in the original study were unduly influenced by the nature of the samples used, the preferences or expectations of the researchers, the geographical location in which a study was conducted, or other such extraneous influences.

Respondent An individual who responds to a questionnaire, an interview, a test, or other kind of instrument.

Response variable A kind of dependent variable obtained from answers to a test, a questionnaire, or an interview. See **dependent/independent variables** concept.

Robustness The extent to which a test of statistical significance yields conclusions that can be trusted even when there are minor violations of the assumptions on which the test is based.

Semi-interquartile range The semi-interquartile range is equal to the interquartile range divided by 2. The interquartile range is a measure of variability calculated by taking the difference between the first and third quartiles (i. e., the 25th and 75th percentiles) of a distribution. See **interquartile range** concept.

Spread Same as variability, dispersion, and scatter.

Squared deviations The square of the differences between the mean and individual measurements in a distribution, i.e., each difference is multiplied by itself. See **Appendix A-16: How to Perform a *t*-Test**.

SS The symbol for *sum of squares*.

Standard error of difference between means The standard deviation of the differences between the means of a large number of samples of the same size from the same population. Can only be estimated when a small number of samples are used. See **Appendix A-16: How to Perform a *t*-Test**.

Statistical accidents Rare statistical events. For example, it is possible, though rare, to get 10 heads in a row in 10 tosses of a coin. Another example: Even in two strictly random samples, it is possible (remotely) that one will have a disproportionate number of young individuals and the other will have a disproportionate number of older persons.

Statistical operations Processes that involve computing statistical values like medians, means, standard deviations, quartiles, tests of statistical significance, confidence intervals, and so forth.

Strata Categories for dividing a population into groups. For example, if college students are divided into groups of freshmen, sophomores, juniors and seniors, each subgroup is a stratum. See **stratified random sample** concept.

Strength of association See strength of relationship.

Strength of relationship The proportion of variance in one variable that accounts for, or is associated with, the variance in another. See **coefficient of determination** concept.

Subject An individual on whom data are collected for analysis in a research study.

Substantive significance Same as practical significance. The extent to which research results are of practical importance, whether statistically significant or not.

Survey A research investigation for obtaining information on individuals in a population to ascertain the status of the group on selected variables. Instruments often used are questionnaires, interviews, attitude scales, and tests.

Symmetrical Distributed (e.g., on both sides) in a similar but inverse way with reference to a given point, as in a mirror image. For example, a distribution that has a very similar form on both sides of the mean. See **normal distribution** concept.

Systematic error An error that consistently distorts all measurements or observations in the same direction, resulting in biased data.

Uncontrolled variable Any influence that can affect research results, and for which there is no plan in the design to account for or assess its impact on conclusions.

Upper real limit The high end of a class interval. See **class interval** concept.

Variability A tendency to vary or change. The extent to which a set of measurements differ from one another.

Within variance estimate The average estimate of the population variance within the groups, with reference to each group's own mean, in an analysis of variance. See **analysis of variance** concept and **Appendix A-17: How to Calculate a One-way Analysis of Variance**.

Index

Note: Items that appear in **boldface** are the major concepts that are defined and illustrated in this book.